Everyday/
Revolutionary

/ How Daniel's Story and Peter's Example
Help You Live as a Christian Today

BIBLE STUDY GUIDE | SIX SESSIONS

J. D. Greear

with Vince Antonucci

H HarperChristian
Resources

Contents

A Note from J. D. Greear

Welcome to the *Everyday Revolutionary Bible Study*. As you begin this journey, I want to share my heart for why I put together this study and what I hope you will gain from going through it. Like you, I've witnessed the tension between living faithfully as a Christian and navigating an increasingly complex cultural landscape. Perhaps you've found yourself wrestling with questions that seem to have no clear answers. Questions such as . . .

When should you speak up and when should you stay silent?

How can you show love to your neighbors while standing firm in your convictions?

What does it mean to be both gracious and truthful in a world that often sees these things as mutually exclusive?

This study guide is designed to help you thoughtfully engage with these challenges. It's not a manual for culture warfare, nor is it a call to compromise. Instead, it's an invitation to explore what it means to live as faithful witnesses in our current moment—whether that's in your workplace, children's school, neighborhood, or even on social media.

In this study, we will begin by looking at the life of Daniel, a Jewish man who managed to be both distinctively faithful and genuinely beloved while living in exile in the foreign culture of Babylon. We will explore how Daniel's story isn't just an ancient tale but a roadmap for Christians, as evidenced by Peter and other New Testament writers using Babylon as a metaphor for the secular world after Jesus' ascension. In fact, Peter's nickname for Rome was "Babylon" (see 1 Peter 5:13). We also discuss the type of gospel Jesus preached and look at ways we can live quietly in this culture while testifying loudly for Christ.

My goal for this study is threefold. First, I want to help you develop practical wisdom for navigating real-world situations. You will move beyond simple formulas to consider the principles that guide your decisions in complex scenarios. Second, I want to equip you with a biblical framework for engaging with cultural differences so you can stand firm in God's truth while maintaining his heart of love for those around you. Third, I want to encourage you to live boldly yet wisely. This isn't about being provocative or confrontational but about learning to be faithful in ways that draw others toward Christ rather than push them away.

Thank you for joining me on this journey. May God give you wisdom and courage as you seek to live faithfully in your own Babylon.

— J. D. Greear

How to Use This Guide

Every day, you face moments of decision. Do you go along with what everyone else is doing even if your heart tells you it's wrong? Do you speak up when you sense someone is trying to lead you and others in a direction that goes against God's Word? Do you speak up *at all* in any situation—or do you just stay silent to keep the peace?

In a culture where tolerance is deemed a virtue and disagreement is frowned upon, many Christians feel trapped between two unsatisfying options: become a confrontational culture warrior or quietly compromise their convictions. But there is another way. One we see in Daniel—a man who remained distinctively faithful yet was beloved even in a hostile culture.

In this study, you will draw from Daniel's experience in Babylon—as well as teachings from Jesus, Paul, and Peter in the New Testament—to explore practical wisdom for navigating today's complex cultural challenges. You will discover how to stand firm in your convictions without becoming combative, show genuine love while maintaining biblical truth, navigate social and political issues with wisdom, and build authentic relationships across differences.

Before you begin, know that there are a few ways you can go through this material. You can experience this study with others in a group (such as a Bible study, Sunday school class, or other gathering), or you can go through the content on your own. Either way, the videos are available to view at any time by following the instructions provided with this study guide.

GROUP STUDY

Each of the sessions in this study are divided into two parts: (1) a group study section and (2) a personal study section. The group study section provides a basic framework on how to open your time together, get the most out of the video content, and discuss the key ideas that were presented in the teaching. Each session includes the following:

- **Welcome:** A short opening note about the topic of the session for you to read on your own before you meet as a group.

- **Connect:** A few icebreaker questions to get you and your group members thinking about the topic and interacting with each other.

- **Watch:** An outline of the key points covered in each video teaching along with space for you to take notes as you watch each session.

- **Discuss:** Questions to help you and your group reflect on the teaching material presented and apply it to your lives.

- **Respond:** A short personal exercise to help reinforce the key ideas.

- **Pray:** A place for you to record prayer requests and praises for the week.

If you are doing this study in a group, make sure you have your own copy of the study guide so you can write down your thoughts, responses, and reflections in the space provided—and so you have access to the videos via streaming. You will also want to have a copy of the *Everyday Revolutionary* book, as reading it alongside this guide will provide you with deeper insights. (See the notes at the beginning of each group session and personal study section on which chapters of the book you should read before the next group session.)

Finally, keep these points in mind:

- **Facilitation:** If you are doing this study in a group, you will want to appoint someone to serve as a facilitator. This person will be responsible for starting the video and keeping track of time during discussions and activities. If *you* have been chosen for this role, there are some resources in the back of this guide that can help you lead your group through the study.

- **Faithfulness:** Your group is a place where tremendous growth can happen as you reflect on the Bible, ask questions, and learn what God is doing in other people's lives. For this reason, be fully committed and attend each session so you can build trust and rapport with the other members.

- **Friendship:** The goal of any small group is to serve as a place where people can share, learn about God, and build friendships. So seek to make your group a "safe place." Be honest about your thoughts and feelings, but also listen carefully to everyone else's thoughts, feelings, and opinions. Keep anything personal that your group members share in confidence so that you can create a community where people can heal, be challenged, and grow spiritually.

If you are going through this study on your own, read the opening Welcome section and reflect on the questions in the Connect section. Watch the video and use the outline provided to help you take notes. Finally, personalize the questions and exercises in the Discuss and Respond sections. Close by recording any requests you want to pray about during the week.

PERSONAL STUDY

The personal study is for you to work through on your own during the week. Each exercise is designed to help you explore the key ideas you uncovered during your group time and delve into passages of Scripture that will help you apply those principles to your life. Go at your own pace, doing a little each day—or tackle the material all at once. Remember to spend a few moments in silence to listen to whatever God might be saying to you.

Note that if you are doing this study as part of a group and you are unable to finish (or even start) these personal studies for the week, you should still attend the group time. Be assured you are still wanted and welcome even if you don't have your "homework" done. The group studies and personal studies are intended to help you hear what God wants you to hear and learn how to apply what he is saying to your life. So . . . as you go through this study, be listening for him to help you know how to live faithfully and courageously in your Babylon.

BEFORE GROUP MEETING	Read chapters 1–3 in *Everyday Revolutionary* Read the Welcome section (page 2)
GROUP MEETING	Discuss the Connect questions Watch the video teaching for session 1 Discuss the questions that follow as a group Do the closing exercise and pray (pages 2–6)
STUDY 1	Complete the personal study (pages 8–11)
STUDY 2	Complete the personal study (pages 12–15)
STUDY 3	Complete the personal study (pages 16–19)
CONNECT AND DISCUSS	Connect with one or two group members Discuss the follow-up questions (page 20)
CATCH UP AND READ AHEAD (BEFORE WEEK 2 GROUP MEETING)	Read chapters 4–6 in *Everyday Revolutionary* Complete any unfinished personal studies (page 21)

Made to Make a Difference

For we are God's handiwork, created in Christ Jesus to do good works, which God prepared in advance for us to do.

EPHESIANS 2:10

WELCOME [READ ON YOUR OWN]

Throughout history, faithful believers have found themselves as strangers in a foreign land. Consider the experience of Makoto Fujimura, an internationally renowned contemporary artist whose work has been exhibited in museums such as the National Gallery in Washington, DC. Rather than creating exclusively "Christian art," Fujimura has engaged the mainstream art world while bringing his distinct faith perspective to his work and cultural leadership.

"Artists are to help us see beyond seeing, to encounter the world with all our senses and intuition," Fujimura wrote in his book *Culture Care*. As founder of the International Arts Movement and former director of the Brehm Center for Worship, Theology, and the Arts, Fujimura has advocated for what he calls "culture care" rather than "culture war"—an approach of nurturing cultural goodness while maintaining Christian distinctiveness. "What would happen if, instead of fighting a 'culture war' to regain a mythic golden past," he asks in his book, "we set about to love our broken world through our broken but creative selves?"[1]

This tension between cultural engagement and faithful distinctiveness has challenged believers throughout church history. The early Christians faced it in Rome, the Reformation believers confronted it in medieval Europe, and missionaries have navigated it in countless global contexts. In each case, those who made the greatest impact maintained their distinctive Christian identity while genuinely loving and serving their communities.

Today, we face our own version of this challenge. As our culture increasingly views Christianity as irrelevant or even harmful, we must discover what it means to be faithfully present without being culturally absorbed. The book of Daniel provides us with a compelling model. Daniel and his friends flourished in Babylon without compromising their core convictions. They earned the respect of kings while maintaining their allegiance to the King of Kings. Their example teaches us that making a difference requires being different—not in superficial ways, but in the fundamental values that shape our lives and choices.

CONNECT [10 MINUTES]

If you or any of your group members don't know each other, take a few minutes to introduce yourselves. Then discuss one or both of the following questions:

- Why did you decide to join this study? What do you hope to learn?

— *or* —

- On a scale of 1 (very easy) to 10 (extremely difficult), how challenging do you find it to maintain your Christian distinctiveness while still engaging positively with those who don't share your faith? Explain your response.

WATCH [25 MINUTES]

Watch the video for this session, which you can access by playing the DVD or through streaming (see the instructions provided with this guide). Below is an outline of the key points covered during the teaching. Record any key concepts that stand out to you.

OUTLINE

I. Christians must navigate a cultural shift that is increasingly hostile to faith.
   - **A.** We have moved from a "positive world" (pre-1994) where Christianity was considered a social asset.
   - **B.** We experienced a "neutral world" (1994–2014) where Christianity was one option among many.
   - **C.** We now live in a "negative world" where Christianity is often considered a social ill.
   - **D.** The biblical books of Daniel and 1 Peter provide guidance for faithful living in this environment.

II. Daniel models how to be faithful in a foreign culture.
   - **A.** The book of Daniel is written primarily in Aramaic, the language of Babylon.
   - **B.** Daniel and his friends were selected for Babylonian education and training.
   - **C.** Their first test came when they were commanded to eat food that violated God's dietary laws.
   - **D.** They remained faithful while still seeking to bless Babylon and its people.

III. Christians in Babylon can expect to be different in their core claims.
   - **A.** Daniel and his friends never got in trouble for private beliefs but for public allegiance.
   - **B.** Christians will face pressure to keep their convictions private.
   - **C.** Like the early Christians, we cannot acknowledge any king but Jesus.
   - **D.** Compromise, not persecution, is what will destroy our witness.

IV. Christians in Babylon are distinct in their guiding values.
   - **A.** Our approach to money is based on generosity, not acquisition.
   - **B.** Our view of power focuses on service rather than self-promotion.
   - **C.** Our understanding of sexuality follows God's design rather than personal preference.
   - **D.** Our distinctiveness should shine like stars in a dark sky, pointing other people to God's kingdom.

NOTES

DISCUSS [35 MINUTES]

Discuss what you just watched by answering the following questions.

1. We have witnessed a cultural shift from a "positive world" to a "negative world" where Christianity is increasingly viewed as harmful. How have you personally experienced this shift? How has it affected your approach to sharing your faith?

2. Daniel and his friends took Babylonian names and received Babylonian education yet remained faithful to God. They participated in the culture of Babylon but did not allow it to compromise their obedience to the Lord. In what ways are Christians today called to do the same? Why is it often so difficult to engage with culture but not allow it to influence you?

3. Ask someone to read aloud Daniel 1:8–15. What principles do you learn from Daniel's approach to maintaining his convictions while still respecting authority? How might this apply to situations you face?

4. Christians are distinct primarily in their approach to money, power, and sexuality. Which of these areas presents the greatest challenge for you? Can you think of an example where a fellow Christian lived such a distinctive life that he or she pointed others to God's kingdom?

5. Invite someone to read Jeremiah 29:4–7. How does God's instruction to the exiles to "seek the peace and prosperity of the city" challenge the way in which you engage with culture today? What might this look like in practical terms?

RESPOND [10 MINUTES]

Living differently from the world as a Christian isn't about wearing peculiar clothing, using unique words, or engaging in social isolation. Rather, it is about living according to the values of God's kingdom while embedded in your culture. Take a few minutes on your own to reflect on this idea as you read the following passages and answer the questions.

> Those who are wise will shine like the brightness of the heavens, and those who lead many to righteousness, like the stars for ever and ever.
>
> **DANIEL 12:3**
>
> But you are a chosen people, a royal priesthood, a holy nation, God's special possession, that you may declare the praises of him who called you out of darkness into his wonderful light. Once you were not a people, but now you are the people of God; once you had not received mercy, but now you have received mercy.
>
> **1 PETER 2:9–10**

How does the image of "shining like stars" relate to the idea of being different in your "Babylon"? What aspects of your life shine most brightly as a testimony to God's kingdom?

Peter describes believers as "a chosen people, a royal priesthood, a holy nation." How might embracing this identity change the way you approach situations where your faith puts you at odds with cultural expectations?

PRAY [10 MINUTES]

As you close, thank God for the example of Daniel and his friends who remained faithful in a foreign land. Ask for wisdom to discern which aspects of your culture you can embrace and which you must resist. Pray for courage to maintain your distinctive Christian witness, especially in areas where it may be costly. Ask that God would help you to genuinely seek the welfare of your community while remaining true to your primary allegiance to Christ.

Personal Study

The goal of this study is to help you and your fellow group members gain a better understanding of what it means to be *in* the world and yet distinctly not *of* it—to be faithfully present with the lost without being absorbed into their culture. What would it look like for you to stand for God's truth but also have compassion and care for your culture rather than being at war with it? As you work through each of these exercises, be sure to write down your responses to the questions. (If you are engaging this study as part of a group, you will be given a few minutes to share your insights at the start of the next session.) If you are reading *Everyday Revolutionary* alongside this study, first review chapters 1–3 of the book.

Daniel Was Different

Imagine being ripped from your homeland as a teenager and sent to a foreign land that wants to erase everything you believe. Your captors don't want you just to obey—they want you to become one of them. They change your name, immerse you in their worldview, and dangle power and privilege before you. The easiest thing to do? Blend in. Adapt. Survive.

This is the situation Daniel faced. Perhaps the real miracle of his life wasn't just that he survived Babylon but that it never swallowed him. He learned the Babylonian language, studied its literature, and even served in its government. Yet he never compromised his allegiance to God. He was a walking contradiction, fully immersed in his culture but never defined by it.

The result? He was both hated and honored. The same king who sentenced him to death in a lion's den (which came about due to hatred from Daniel's opponents) spent the whole night pacing in distress, hoping his God would save him. Daniel's faithfulness made him a target, but his integrity made him indispensable.

The same challenge confronts you today. The pressure will not come from a Babylonian king but possibly from a corporate policy that clashes with biblical truth, or a university classroom that ridicules faith, or a social circle that equates conviction with intolerance. Will you stand firm? Or will you quietly conform?

The temptation is to take one of two extremes: withdraw from culture entirely or compromise your convictions to fit in. Daniel shows a better way. He proves you can be deeply engaged in the world—excelling in your work, building relationships, and contributing to your community—while remaining unshakably faithful to God's truth.

This kind of cultural engagement requires wisdom, courage, and deep spiritual maturity. It means knowing when to cooperate and when to resist. It means standing firm in your convictions without arrogance and extending love without compromise. It means living in a way that makes the world stop and take notice.

Daniel didn't just survive Babylon—he shaped it. And so can you. The world doesn't need more Christians who retreat in fear or blend in without conviction. It needs people like Daniel—bold, wise, faithful. People whose presence is undeniable, whose integrity is unshakable, and whose lives point unmistakably to the God they serve.

Read | Daniel 6:1–5, 6–9, 19–23

1. What stands out to you about the way Daniel interacted with Babylonian culture at the beginning of this story (see 6:1–5)? What did he accept and what did he reject?

2. Why do you think the officials specifically chose prayer as the activity to ban rather than some other religious practice (see verses 6–9)? What does this suggest about what they understood about Daniel's faith?

Daniel leads not one but two Babylonian kings to recognize the God of Israel (see Daniel 2:27-47; 5:17-29). Daniel didn't fit in—often awkwardly and dangerously so. He was so countercultural that he got thrown into a lion's den . . . yet so beloved, at the same time, that the king whose decree put him there stayed awake all night distressed that he might have lost him (see Daniel 6). This raises questions for me. How do we become like that in our society? How can we live with Daniel's courage and yet be so beloved by our communities that they loathe the thought of our departure?[2]

3. Daniel stood out not only for going against the norms of Babylonian society but also for his character and integrity. Could people say the same of you? Rate how those who know you well might respond to how you "stand out" in the following areas:

Never cutting corners:

O—O—O—O—O—O—O—O—O—O
[same as everyone else]   [completely different]

Maintaining integrity even in the small things:

O—O—O—O—O—O—O—O—O—O
[same as everyone else]   [completely different]

Standing up for what God values:

O—O—O—O—O—O—O—O—O—O
[same as everyone else]   [completely different]

4. In Daniel 6:19–23, Daniel greets the king with "May the king live forever!"—a respectful address—even though the king's decree had put him in danger. He also affirms he had "done no wrong" before the king. How does Daniel's response reveal the tension between honoring human authority and remaining faithful to God when the two are in conflict?

I'm concerned about the direction our society is going, but I believe God has us here for a reason. I'm convinced that he intends to do some profound things in us and through us in the coming generation. There will be fiery furnaces and lion's dens, for sure. And those aren't fun, to say the least. But there's also a God in heaven who shuts the mouths of lions, quenches the violence of fire, and changes the hearts of pagan kings. The "Babylons" in which we are placed should have no one who loves them more, even as it's clear that we disagree with so much of what they stand for. At times we'll make them so mad they want to throw us into the lion's den. Even they will be surprised, however, when they find themselves outside the den hoping against hope that we make it through the night.[3]

5. How might our "Babylons" (workplaces, communities, or cultural institutions) benefit from Christians who love them deeply even while disagreeing with certain values? How can you demonstrate this kind of principled love in your world today?

Our Message Is Subversive

Imagine waking up to find your beliefs reclassified—not just as outdated but as dangerous. What was once common sense is now extremist. What was once a moral conviction is now called hate.

This shift mirrors what Daniel, Esther, and the early Christians faced. The Babylonians saw the Jewish faith as a threat. The Romans labeled Christians "atheists" for refusing to worship Caesar and "anarchists" for pledging allegiance to a greater King. Time and again, God's people were painted as obstacles to progress—yet their faith outlasted empires.

Today, we face the same moment. Core truths—Christ's exclusivity, sin's reality, the call to repentance, God's design for gender and sexuality—are seen not just as wrong but also as oppressive. We now live outside the "Overton window," the sociological term for ideas deemed unacceptable in public discourse.

But this isn't failure—it's authenticity. Jesus warned, "If the world hates you, keep in mind that it hated me first" (John 15:18). The question isn't *whether* we will face opposition but how we will *respond* to it. Like Daniel, we must be "bilingual and bicultural"—engaging our culture wisely while staying unshakably faithful.

Some battles require adaptation, like Daniel mastering Babylonian customs. Others require bold resistance, like refusing to compromise worship. The real question isn't just what we will say but how will we stand. Will we compromise to keep the peace? Withdraw to avoid conflict? Or, like Daniel, will we engage with wisdom, truth, and unwavering faith?

The gospel is meant to be subversive. Stripping it of offense would strip it of power. The challenge isn't to make it palatable but visible—to show that this "dangerous" message brings life, not harm; freedom, not oppression; healing, not despair.

The world calls our faith *dangerous*. Let's show them it's dangerous in the best way—dangerous to corruption, despair, and the lies that enslave. We're not here to retreat. We're here to shine. And the darker it gets, the brighter the light of Christ will be.

Read | John 15:18–19; Acts 17:6–7; 1 Peter 2:11–12

1. Jesus said the world hates his followers because he "chose [them] out of the world" (John 15:19). How can remembering that you are *chosen* by Jesus reshape the way you view opposition—and help you respond with grace instead of bitterness?

2. Jesus' message was seen as a threat to political order rather than a source of spiritual truth (see Acts 17:6–7). How are Christian beliefs still misunderstood or misrepresented today? How can you respond with wisdom, clarity, and grace when your faith is distorted?

Growing up in church, we used to sing a song called "Jesus Is the Answer." For most Americans today, Jesus is not only *not* the answer, but he and his people are also the *problem*. I'm hesitant to use the term *persecution* to describe this new situation, especially in light of what followers of Jesus in other parts of the world experience. I'd prefer to leave the term *persecution* for them. In the West we are experiencing *marginalization*, however, and that is no small thing. Marginalization has many deleterious effects, particularly for those trying to make a living in Babylon, and marginalization is often the precursor to persecution. This new reality is indeed tragic. But here's the point: *the new reality changes the rules of engagement.*[4]

3. How might you be contributing to how non-Christians view Christians? Consider how you typically react to the following challenges.

Challenges	Undesired Response	Desired Response
When my beliefs are challenged	Get defensive	Listen first, then respond with grace
When facing opposition	Withdraw to safe Christian circles	Stay engaged while maintaining boundaries
When feeling misunderstood	React with anger	Seek to understand others' perspectives
When values clash	Argue to win	Share truth with gentleness

Where do you see the biggest gap between your usual response and your desired response? What steps could you take to move toward your desired response in that area?

4. Peter urges us to live such "good lives" that even those who criticize us will glorify God (1 Peter 2:12). Rather than watering down the gospel to make it more palatable, how can you make it more visible? What real-life expressions—like acts of service, integrity, or selfless love—can help skeptical observers see the beauty of Christ through you today?

Peter envisions us living right in the middle of Babylon in a way that is remarkably attractive. So attractive, in fact, that Babylonians feel compelled to ask the reason for it. Peter doesn't envision our "peculiarity" manifesting itself because of our pushy God-talk, our "bless you, brothers" or because we defiantly correct the Starbucks barista with "Merry Christmas" whenever she says "Happy Holidays." I'm not saying you should never do that, just that Peter's point is that by working faithfully, honestly, and *quietly*—seeking peace and conducting our lives with gentleness and respect—our lives will be so remarkably beautiful that Babylonians will feel compelled to inquire about the source of that beauty. God's plan to change the world through us focuses not on political activism but on his exiles living quiet, beautiful lives accompanied by clear gospel testimony.[5]

5. What changes could you make to your daily life to better embody this "remarkably attractive" way of living that Peter describes in 1 Peter 2:11–12? What is one specific act of service you could commit to doing this week?

Our Values Are Upside-Down

Imagine stepping into an art gallery and finding every masterpiece hanging upside down. Your stomach tightens. Your mind protests. Skies stretch beneath rolling hills. Rivers flow in reverse. Portraits show dignified figures standing on their heads. It feels wrong. Unnatural, even. Your first instinct? Someone made a mistake. These paintings should be flipped back, right?

But what if the artist did this on purpose? What if, by flipping the world upside down, the artist was actually showing you how to see it *right-side up* for the first time?

This is how God's kingdom works. In God's kingdom, everything the world calls "right" is often upside-down. The first become last. The weak overpower the strong. Those who surrender win the greatest battles. The greatest throne was a cross. What looks like failure often carries the seeds of eternal victory.

But these upside-down values don't just exist in theory—they redefine how you live every day. The world says power is found at the top, but God does his best work in the margins. Society says that success means climbing higher, yet Jesus knelt lower. The culture celebrates moving up to first class, but some of God's greatest assignments happen in coach.

That demotion at work? It might be God's promotion into a new mission field—one you never would have chosen but desperately need. That rejection from a friend? It might be the very place God wants your faith to shine brightest, teaching you to love without condition. That position with less prestige? It could be your strategic assignment in God's kingdom, where unseen faithfulness builds eternal reward.

When you embrace God's upside-down economy, you stop measuring success the way the world does. Instead of asking, "How can I move up?" you ask, "Where is God already at work?" Instead of lamenting your lack of influence, you recognize that God's power is often made perfect in weakness. Instead of striving for the "right" circles, you realize that God often places you in the "wrong" place for his right purposes.

Like an upside-down masterpiece, God's kingdom doesn't just change how you see—it changes how you *live*. The question is: Will you keep trying to flip his design to fit your comfort, or will you let him turn your world upside down . . . so you can finally see right-side up?

Read | 1 Corinthians 1:26–31; 7:26–31; 3:18–20

1. When you consider your gifts, background, and limitations, how has God used what the world considers "foolish" or "weak" about you to accomplish his purposes (see 1 Corinthians 1:26–31)? What might this reveal about God's wisdom and the way he works?

2. In 1 Corinthians 7:26–31, Paul speaks into a time of "present crisis" (likely persecution or social upheaval) and, in that context, encourages believers to remain in their current situation. Why do you think Paul gave this advice? How might staying where they were help them be more faithful to Jesus and more influential for his kingdom?

One of the things we find as we read the Bible is that in the worst moments of Christian history, God was doing a different thing than what everyone expected, a *better* thing, even though it was a *different* thing than what they wanted. When Jesus commissioned this church, he gave them the assignment to carry the gospel to the ends of the earth. They were to start in Jerusalem, move to Judea, then to Samaria, and finally to the uttermost parts of the earth (see Acts 1:8). So, as awesome as those first few months of church life were, they were still only in phase 1 of what God wanted to do. God sent the persecution to fulfill his plans, and this group of scattered believers planted churches in Judea, Samaria, and eventually to the ends of the earth. What the disciples wanted in Jerusalem (a thriving church in a peaceful context) was a *good* thing, it just wasn't what God wanted. God wanted to put witnesses in Babylons around the world.[6]

3. Just as God had more in store for the early church beyond "phase one," he may be using changes in your life to prepare you for what is next—even if you don't see it yet. God may have something better for you than what you have planned! Write down some examples of where you're currently experiencing change. How might God be using these changes to move you into the next phase of his purpose for you?

> Professional Life:

> Community Status:

> Church Role:

> Family and Friendships:

You are in that profession, or living in that neighborhood, or on that particular hall, or sitting next to that particular person, for a reason. Your successes *and* failures put you into contact with particular groups of people that God is seeking. Wherever you are, God has determined *your* place—the borders of where you live and who you know. He has sovereignly directed the choices, successes, and failures that brought you there. He did that because he is at work in the people around you, putting questions and problems in their lives so they might seek him. And he brought them up next to you. So, rather than resisting his will, why not pray for those in your Babylon? You never know when you'll discover your heavenly Father powerfully at work.[7]

4. What current situation in your life feels like a disadvantage that God might actually be using for his purposes? What opportunities for advancing his kingdom exist in your current position that might not be available if you were in a more "prominent" place?

5. Paul writes, "Do not deceive yourselves. If any of you think you are wise by the standards of this age, you should become 'fools' so that you may become wise" (1 Corinthians 3:18). What specific "wisdom" in our current culture might you need to reject in order to embrace God's wisdom? Can you think of an example that especially applies to your life?

Connect and Discuss

Take some time today to connect with a fellow group member and discuss some of the key insights from this session. Use any of the following prompts to help guide your discussion.

What did you like best from the content in this session, including both the group study and personal study? Why?

What inspires you about Daniel's example in the Bible?

How is God using you in the places he has put you? What might be some new ways he can use you that you haven't embraced yet?

Do you have any fears about doing this study or the changes it may lead you to make in your life? If so, what are those fears?

What do you feel most excited to explore in the sessions ahead? Why?

Catch Up and Read Ahead

Use this time to go back and complete any of the study and reflection questions from previous days that you weren't able to finish. Make a note below of any revelations you've had and reflect on any growth or personal insights you've gained.

Read chapters 4–6 in *Everyday Revolutionary* before the next group gathering. Use the space below to make note of anything in those chapters that stands out to you or encourages you.

BEFORE GROUP MEETING	Read chapters 4–6 in *Everyday Revolutionary* Read the Welcome section (page 24)
GROUP MEETING	Discuss the Connect questions Watch the video teaching for session 2 Discuss the questions that follow as a group Do the closing exercise and pray (pages 24–28)
STUDY 1	Complete the personal study (pages 30–33)
STUDY 2	Complete the personal study (pages 34–37)
STUDY 3	Complete the personal study (pages 38–41)
CONNECT AND DISCUSS	Connect with one or two group members Discuss the follow-up questions (page 42)
CATCH UP AND READ AHEAD (BEFORE WEEK 3 GROUP MEETING)	Read chapter 7 in *Everyday Revolutionary* Complete any unfinished personal studies (page 43)

Why We Are Here

*Preach the word; be prepared in season and
out of season; correct, rebuke and encourage—
with great patience and careful instruction.*

2 TIMOTHY 4:2

WELCOME [READ ON YOUR OWN]

In 2010, Wangari Maathai, the first African woman to receive the Nobel Peace Prize, told what has since become known as "The Hummingbird Story." In the parable, a forest fire breaks out and all the animals flee to the edge of the woods, watching helplessly as their homes burn. They feel powerless against the enormous blaze.

All except for one tiny hummingbird. This small bird flies to the nearest stream, picks up a drop of water in its beak, flies back to the fire, and drops it on the flames. It repeats the action again and again. The other animals—including the elephants, who could carry more water—watch in bewilderment. "What are you doing?" they ask mockingly. "You're too small! Your tiny drops won't put out this fire!" The hummingbird, without pausing in its work, looks back and says, "I'm doing what I can."

Maathai used this story to illustrate how people can make a difference in the face of seemingly insurmountable challenges. The hummingbird didn't stop to calculate whether its efforts would be sufficient to extinguish the entire fire. It simply understood its purpose in that moment and acted accordingly.[8]

Like the hummingbird, we often find ourselves in a world consumed by various "fires"—injustice, poverty, moral decay, polarization. The scale of these problems can feel overwhelming, leading some of us to retreat into isolation while others among us become consumed by political or cultural battles, forgetting our primary purpose.

But what if, like the hummingbird, our effectiveness isn't measured by whether we solve the world's problems but by our faithfulness to our specific calling? What if our primary purpose isn't to "put out the fire" through political or cultural domination but to faithfully witness to the truth and character of Jesus?

This is what you will explore in this session—what Jesus said about why you're really here and what your main focus should be as you engage with the world around you.

CONNECT [10 MINUTES]

If you or any of your group members don't know each other, take a few minutes to introduce yourselves. Then discuss one or both of the following questions:

- What is something that spoke to you in last week's personal study that you would like to share with the group?

— *or* —

- Why do you think it's so easy for Christians to ignore their primary calling of being witnesses of Jesus who make disciples?

WATCH [25 MINUTES]

Now watch the video for this session. Below is an outline of the main points covered during the teaching. Record any key concepts that stand out to you.

OUTLINE

I. Christians often misunderstand why God has placed them in the world.
  A. We often mistake political engagement as our primary purpose.
  B. We can become fixated on cultural battles rather than our core mission.
  C. Many of us assume our purpose is to "bring in the kingdom" through our efforts.

II. Jesus clarified our purpose in Acts 1 before his ascension.
  A. The disciples asked about restoring the kingdom to Israel.
  B. Jesus redirected their focus away from timing and political restoration.
  C. He emphasized receiving power to be his witnesses.
  D. Our primary identity is as witnesses, not kingdom-builders.

III. Our role is to provide signs that point to Jesus' kingdom.
  A. Signs are temporary and point to something beyond themselves.
  B. Jesus' miracles were signs of the kingdom, not the full kingdom itself.
  C. As Christians, we demonstrate kingdom realities through our lives and actions.
  D. Our purpose is to present an accurate picture of Jesus and his coming kingdom.

IV. Effective witness requires both truth and grace.
  A. The Great Commission centers on making disciples, not just winning arguments.
  B. Our communities should experience joy because of our presence.
  C. Being faithful witnesses means serving tangible needs in Jesus' name.
  D. True success is measured by accurately representing Jesus in both word and deed.

NOTES

DISCUSS [35 MINUTES]

Discuss what you just watched by answering the following questions.

1. Think about the opening anecdote in the teaching about different Christians meeting with the president. Why is it so easy to confuse political engagement with our primary purpose in this manner? What problems might doing so create for our witness?

2. Invite someone to read Acts 1:6–8. How did Jesus respond to his followers when they asked whether he was about to restore the kingdom to Israel? What different metric did he give them for how to meaningfully engage with the world?

3. Jesus told his followers they would be his "witnesses" (Acts 1:8). How does this identity differ from being fixers, saviors, or cultural warriors? What might it look like to approach today's challenges with the humility of a witness rather than the authority of a ruler?

4. In the teaching, J. D. described how his church engaged with a struggling elementary school. What principles from this story could serve as a guide for how you could engage with the needs in your communities so you can be an effective witness for Jesus?

5. Ask someone to read John 1:14. What do you think it would look like for a Christian (or a church) to be "full of grace and truth"? How might doing so shape the way that body of believers witnesses for Jesus in an increasingly polarized culture?

RESPOND [10 MINUTES]

Jesus made it clear that your primary purpose in this world is to be his witness—to testify to who he is and what his kingdom is like. This means you are representing Jesus not only in what you say but also in how you live and serve. Reflect on this truth as you read the following passages and then answer the questions that follow.

> "You are the salt of the earth. But if the salt loses its saltiness, how can it be made salty again? It is no longer good for anything, except to be thrown out and trampled underfoot."
>
> **MATTHEW 5:13**

> "You are the light of the world. A town built on a hill cannot be hidden. Neither do people light a lamp and put it under a bowl. Instead they put it on its stand, and it gives light to everyone in the house. In the same way, let your light shine before others, that they may see your good deeds and glorify your Father in heaven."
>
> **MATTHEW 5:14-16**

Jesus described his followers as "salt of the earth" and "light of the world." Salt only makes a difference when it makes contact. In the ancient world, it preserved, purified, and enhanced flavor. What is Jesus therefore saying when he says we should be "salt of the earth"?

Jesus said, "A town built on a hill cannot be hidden." What pressures do you often face to hide or downplay your faith? How have you overcome these pressures?

PRAY [10 MINUTES]

As you close this session, pray for clarity about your purpose as a witness for Christ. Ask God to help you avoid being distracted by secondary issues and to keep your primary mission in focus. Pray for opportunities to demonstrate both grace and truth in your community and for the power of the Holy Spirit to make your witness effective. Ask God to help you evaluate your words and actions by how accurately they represent Jesus to those around you.

Personal Study

God calls you to be distinct—because you can't make a difference if you're not different. God wants to work *in* you through the power of the Holy Spirit so that you will be shaped more and more into the likeness of Jesus. He also wants to work *through* you so that instead of being shaped by the culture, you will help shape it. How does that happen? This is what you will be studying this week. As you work through these exercises, continue to write down your responses to the questions. (If you are engaging this study as part of a group, you will be given a few minutes to share your insights at the start of the next session.) If you are reading *Everyday Revolutionary* alongside this study, first review chapters 4–6 of the book.

The Power of the Holy Spirit

It's fascinating to watch a master craftsperson at work. The potter's hands press into the soft clay, shaping it with just the right amount of pressure—never crushing but only guiding. The woodworker runs a hand over the grain before making a single cut, knowing that working against it will ruin the design. The glassblower moves with precision, every breath and motion timed perfectly, knowing that too much force will shatter the masterpiece.

This is how the Holy Spirit works in us—not with coercion but with careful, intentional power. He doesn't force or manipulate; rather, he shapes, refines, and transforms. His power is not like the world's—grasping for control, demanding submission—but a power that works from the inside out, changing hearts and, through them, entire communities.

When Jesus told his disciples, "You will receive power when the Holy Spirit comes upon you" (Acts 1:8 NLT), he wasn't giving them a promise of political dominance or social control. He was giving them something far greater—the power to bear witness to a kingdom not of this world. A power not of force, but of faithfulness. Not of control, but of conviction.

And yet, this power often looks upside down. It's the power of a believer who forgives when the world says to retaliate, serves when others grasp for influence, and speaks truth not with volume and outrage but with courage and grace. It's the power to love your enemies, to bless those who curse you, and to choose humility when pride would be easier.

The world defines power as the ability to make others do what you want. The Holy Spirit's power, by contrast, makes you more like Jesus—and through you, he reveals himself to others. This is a power that allows a handful of ordinary people to transform entire communities through active engagement and faithful presence. It's a power that sustains joy in suffering, love in the face of hostility, and hope in seemingly hopeless situations. This is the power we are called to live out in our modern Babylons. Not by chasing influence or demanding control but by embodying the gospel—proving that Jesus changes everything.

So, where is the Spirit calling you to live differently? In your workplace? Your home? Your relationships? How will you display his power today—not by force, but by faithfulness?

Read | 1 Corinthians 2:1–5; 2 Corinthians 12:9–10; Acts 1:4–8

1. Paul describes himself coming to the Corinthians "in weakness and in fear and much trembling" (1 Corinthians 2:3 ESV) and later boasts in his weaknesses (see 2 Corinthians 12:9). How is this approach different from what we often see exhibited by leaders today? What does this say about the means you should employ to influence your world?

2. Paul says the effectiveness of his message depends on the demonstration of God's power rather than his own wisdom or rhetoric (see 1 Corinthians 2:4–5). How should this same attitude affect how you live and share the message of Jesus?

> We influence and shape the earthly kingdoms we're a part of, but our primary kingdom is not of this world. We testify to it and give signs of it, but we don't bring it in its fullness. Before Jesus ascended back to heaven, his disciples asked him, "Lord, are you at this time going to restore the kingdom to Israel?" (Acts 1:6). The disciples were asking about the timeline for establishing Jesus' *political* kingdom and what they might do to help bring it about. Jesus basically said to them, "That's not your concern. When I return is under the Father's control. For now, my power is coming upon you to testify."[9]

3. In Acts 1:4–8, Jesus redirects the disciples from speculation about the times and seasons when God will restore the kingdom to certainty about their current task and mission. In what areas of your life might you be focusing on questions that God hasn't yet answered while overlooking the clear calling that he has provided to you?

4. Look at the disciples' preoccupation with timing and restoration in Acts 1:6 and Jesus' answer about their primary mission in verses 7–8. What does this contrast reveal about the misconceptions Christians often have about how God's kingdom advances on earth?

We have a gospel too precious and a mission too urgent to let *anything* stand in its way. Forfeiting opportunities for that mission so we can engage in some form of nation-building confuses our role in Babylon and hinders our mission. Robert Woodberry, during his PhD studies in sociology at the University of North Carolina, made a startling discovery regarding the history of Protestant missions. He found that most of the missionaries didn't set out to be political activists. They were first and foremost people who loved other people. They cared about other people, saw that they'd been wronged, and wanted to make it right. The missionaries didn't come primarily as systemic reformers, they came primarily as evangelists, witnesses, and disciple-makers. As they encountered suffering, however, they felt compelled to relieve it. Most importantly, as they taught the gospel, their converts developed their own yearnings for justice. The transforming power of the gospel inevitably led to societal change.[10]

5. True gospel transformation naturally produces "yearnings for justice" in new believers. How has your own spiritual growth changed your perspective on social issues? What specific injustices do you feel particularly called to address as a result of your faith?

Live in Beloved Community

Every generation of Christians wrestles with the same challenge of how to *stand out* without *standing apart* . . . to be different without being dismissed as irrelevant or strange. The pressure to blend in—to conform to cultural values and priorities—is relentless. But our calling isn't to retreat or rebel. It's to be distinct in a way that captivates, not alienates.

Many Christians have tried to signal their faith through surface-level distinctives—rigid dress codes, strict music preferences, or cultural withdrawal. But these external markers often miss the heart of what it means to be set apart. True Christian distinctiveness isn't about *looking* different but about *living* differently.

The difference to which Jesus calls us is radical yet deeply attractive. It is seen in how we handle money, power, and relationships. When we choose generosity over accumulation, service over dominance, and self-giving love over self-protection, we embody a way of life that is both countercultural and compelling. This kind of distinctiveness creates curiosity.

The early church wasn't known for its dress code but for its radical generosity, its care for the sick and poor, and its refusal to live by the empire's values. People took notice—not because Christians withdrew, but because they engaged the world differently. Living in beloved community thus means being different in ways that invite rather than repel. Our distinctiveness should reflect the beauty of God's kingdom, not create unnecessary barriers to it. Like the moon reflecting the sun's light, we shine not by overpowering but by illuminating.

This isn't just about grand gestures. The power of our witness is proven in the everyday: in how we treat employees, how we spend our weekends, how we use our resources, and how we respond to those in need. These daily choices—not rules or restrictions—reveal whether we truly belong to another kingdom.

So, does your life stand out in ways that invite people in rather than keep them out? Are you one who makes a mark not by drawing lines that separate but by drawing lines that attract people to Christ? Remember, the most compelling evidence of God's kingdom is a community so distinct, so loving, so generous that the world can't help but take notice.

Read | Romans 12:1–2; Philippians 2:14–16; Titus 2:7–8

1. In Romans 12:1–2, Paul warns against conforming to "the pattern of this world." What particular worldly pattern or value have you noticed yourself unconsciously adopting? How has this affected your spiritual life?

2. Paul says you will "shine like stars" when you hold firmly to the word of life (see Philippians 2:14–16). What does holding firmly to God's Word look like in your daily routine? How might you strengthen this grip in practical ways?

Tim Keller notes, "The early church was strikingly different from the culture around it in this way: the pagan society was stingy with its money and promiscuous with its body. A pagan gave nobody their money and practically gave everybody their body. And the Christians came along and gave practically nobody their body and they gave practically everybody their money." In other words, while Babylonians are promiscuous with their beds and guarded with their money, Christian exiles are promiscuous with their money and guarded with their beds. Followers of Jesus just look different. That's because we shape our lives according to fundamentally different values. When we do that, we won't need a distinctive haircut or alternative music style to "come out from among them and be ye separate." We will be as distinct from Babylon as light is from darkness, even when we're dressed in Babylonian clothes and called by Babylonian names."

3. As a follower of Jesus, your life should look different from the world because it is shaped by different values. How is your life proving to be different in these areas?

How I am different in the way I use money and resources . . .

How I am different in the way I use power and influence . . .

How I am different in the way I interact with others . . .

4. Paul instructs Titus that he should set "an example by doing what is good" so that those who oppose him will "be ashamed because they have nothing bad to say" (Titus 2:7–8). Think about how non-Christians might perceive your faith. What aspect of your conduct might give them legitimate reason to criticize Christianity? How could you address this?

Like Daniel, believers in Babylon today will be tested. In lots of places and in lots of ways. Places we are tested are as unique as the places we find ourselves in. And we can expect setbacks along the way. Sure, Daniel and his friends prospered, but they faced a lot of angry kings, fiery furnaces, and lion's dens along the way. We will too. But God has already determined that his kingdom wins in the end. When we glow with kingdom values, we assure the world the resurrected Jesus is returning soon. Our setbacks are only temporary. King Jesus wins in the end. That's been true in every generation, and it will be true in ours too. He stands ready to validate his kingdom in our generation, but he only does so through those willing to set themselves apart from the kingdom of Babylon. If we want to make a difference, we have to be different.[12]

5. Consider the statement that "our setbacks are only temporary." What are some of the setbacks you have endured as you've sought to honor God with your life? What has God revealed to you about himself and his presence through those setbacks?

Be a Witness to the Resurrection

When runners compete in a race, they not only need speed but also direction. Imagine if the lead runners in a race—muscles burning, legs pounding—took a wrong turn. No matter how fast they ran, they wouldn't win if they didn't get back on the right path.

As Christians, our effectiveness isn't just about passion or commitment. It's also about staying on the right course. And yet, countless voices urge us to take detours. Some call us to withdraw and wait for God to intervene while we sit on the sidelines. Others push us to political activism, as if the kingdom of God depended on votes and policies. Still others make our mission about denouncing culture—more known for what we stand against than whom we stand for. None of these ways represent the path Jesus has set before us.

Our *true* calling is to be witnesses to the resurrection of Jesus. In Paul's first letter to the church in Corinth, he wrote that he wanted to remind the believers of the gospel he had preached to them (see 1 Corinthians 15:1–2). He then went on to describe this gospel: "that Christ died for our sins according to the Scriptures, that he was buried, that he was raised on the third day according to the Scriptures" (verses 3–4). Paul didn't see his mission as being about seizing power or withdrawing from culture but simply about testifying to a risen King.

Note that being a witness isn't just about *speaking* truth. It's about *embodying* it. Jesus was "full of grace and truth" (John 1:14), and so must we be. Like the moon reflecting the sun, we shine by reflecting the beauty and power of Christ. This kind of witness can only happen through a transformed life. It happens when we love our cities like Jesus loved Jerusalem, when we serve our communities as he served, and when we are compassionate to those on the fringes of society—just as Jesus was with sinners and outcasts.

If we lose focus in this—if we make the secondary issues the primary ones—we will risk being like those lead runners in the race who take a wrong turn. Instead, we must stay on track and stick to the course, living with grace and truth as we testify to the incredible life found in the risen Jesus. When we do this, we will truly be running the race that *Jesus* has set before us.

Read | Romans 10:11–15; Colossians 4:2–6; 1 Corinthians 13:1–3

1. Paul describes the feet of those who bring good news as "beautiful" (see Romans 10:11–15). In what ways have you experienced the beauty of being God's messenger? When have you missed opportunities to be those "beautiful feet" for someone else?

2. Paul instructs you to be "wise in the way you act toward outsiders" and to let your conversation "be always full of grace, seasoned with salt" (Colossians 4:5–6). Think about some of your recent interactions with non-believers. How might your words or actions have tasted to them—bitter, bland, or seasoned with salt? Explain your response.

"Jesus came to them and said, 'All authority in heaven and on earth has been given to me. Therefore go and make disciples of all nations, baptizing them in the name of the Father and of the Son and of the Holy Spirit, teaching them to observe everything I have commanded you. And surely

I am with you always, to the very end of the age'" (Matthew 28:18-20). Navigators founder Dawson Trotman points out that Jesus uses only one verb in that commission: *mathēteusate*, or "make disciples."[13] Everything else in that sentence that looks like a verb to us (i.e. *go, baptize, teach*) are participles. "So what?" you say. In Greek, that indicates the actions conveyed by the participles flow out of, and anchor themselves in, the verb. In other words, the center of everything the church does is make disciples. All our other activities—our "participles," so to speak—flow out of, and find their legitimacy in, that one central assignment.[14]

3. The Great Commission is not only the mission of the "church" but also the mission of every Christian. Is making disciples the priority in your life that Jesus intends it to be? If not, what might help you become a more intentional and effective disciple-maker?

4. Paul writes of the lost, "How can they hear without someone preaching to them?" (Romans 10:14). Consider your sphere of influence—your family, friends, workplace, and neighborhood. Who might *never* hear about Jesus in these realms of your life unless *you* share the message? Take a few moments to write down some names that come to mind.

In your family . . .

Among your friends . . .

In your workplace . . .

In your neighborhood . . .

It's not enough to merely speak the truth. The life-giving glory of Jesus consists of truth *and* grace. Truth without grace is damning fundamentalism; grace without truth is empty sentimentality. Truth without grace makes you a bully; grace without truth makes you a coward. Truth without grace makes you a culture war hero for the right; grace without truth makes you a beloved religious pundit for the mainstream media. Both are worthless in bringing salvation. Worse than worthless, actually . . . *deadly*. Like sodium and chloride, truth or grace taken in isolation kills. Put them together, however, and they become gospel salt, a life-giving, flavor-inducing preservative.[15]

5. Paul writes in 1 Corinthians 13:1–3 that without love, our words are just a "resounding gong." When has someone shared truth you needed to hear—but without love? How did it make you feel? How might that experience shape the way you speak truth to others?

Connect and Discuss

Take some time today to connect with a fellow group member and discuss some of the key insights from this session. Use any of the following prompts to help guide your discussion.

What did you like best from the content in this session, including both the group study and personal study? Why that content?

What did you learn this week about how God wants to use the power of the Holy Spirit to shape you into someone more distinctive?

What in particular did you learn this week about how God wants to use you to shape the culture around you?

What are some areas in which you want to grow when it comes to being committed to and effective in your mission of making disciples?

What do you feel most excited to explore in the sessions ahead?

Catch Up and Read Ahead

Use this time to go back and complete any of the study and reflection questions from previous days that you weren't able to finish. Make a note below of any revelations you've had and reflect on any growth or personal insights you've gained.

Read chapter 7 in *Everyday Revolutionary* before the next group gathering. Use the space below to make note of anything in those chapters that stands out to you or encourages you.

BEFORE GROUP MEETING	Read chapter 7 in *Everyday Revolutionary* Read the Welcome section (page 46)
GROUP MEETING	Discuss the Connect questions Watch the video teaching for session 3 Discuss the questions that follow as a group Do the closing exercise and pray (pages 46–50)
STUDY 1	Complete the personal study (pages 52–55)
STUDY 2	Complete the personal study (pages 56–59)
STUDY 3	Complete the personal study (pages 60–63)
CONNECT AND DISCUSS	Connect with one or two group members Discuss the follow-up questions (page 64)
CATCH UP AND READ AHEAD (BEFORE WEEK 4 GROUP MEETING)	Read chapters 8–9 in *Everyday Revolutionary* Complete any unfinished personal studies (page 65)

Citizens of Another Kingdom

You are no longer foreigners and strangers,
but fellow citizens with God's people and
also members of his household.

EPHESIANS 2:19

WELCOME [READ ON YOUR OWN]

In 1793, William Carey, a cobbler from rural England, arrived in India as a missionary. He went to preach the gospel, having told his supporters, "Expect great things from God; attempt great things for God." For Carey, the "great thing" was making disciples of Jesus Christ. Yet his legacy extends far beyond evangelism alone.

At one point, Carey witnessed the practice of *sati*, where widows were burned alive on their husbands' funeral pyres. Rather than viewing this as a cultural practice that should be tolerated, or focusing exclusively on disciple-making, Caren advocated tirelessly with the British authorities for its abolition. After years of effort, his advocacy led to the Bengal Sati Regulation Act of 1829, which outlawed the practice. Carey also championed women's education in a society where it was virtually nonexistent and established the first degree-awarding college in Asia.

What is striking about William Carey is how he managed to maintain balance in his life. He never lost sight of his primary calling to make disciples through sharing the gospel. In fact, he translated the Bible into multiple Indian languages. Yet he also understood that genuine love for people meant addressing their physical and social needs alongside their spiritual ones. He operated as a faithful witness to Jesus while engaging with political structures to create lasting change.[16]

Carey's example offers us wisdom for today. Like him, we navigate in a society where political tensions and social challenges abound. Carey shows us a middle path between making political activism our primary focus and avoiding engagement altogether. We can remain focused on our primary identity as witnesses to Jesus while wisely engaging political and social structures. The gospel of Christ has profound implications for all aspects of life, including politics, but always with the kingdom of God as our ultimate loyalty.

CONNECT [10 MINUTES]

Get the session started by choosing one or both of the following questions to discuss together as a group:

- What is something that spoke to you in last week's personal study that you would like to share with the group?

— *or* —

- What was your family's approach to political discussions when you were growing up? Were politics discussed openly, avoided entirely, or something in between?

WATCH [25 MINUTES]

Now watch the video for this session. Below is an outline of the main points covered during the teaching. Record any key concepts that stand out to you.

OUTLINE

I. Christians can fall into the ditch of making earthly politics too important.
  A. Jesus often withdrew from political opportunities to focus on his primary mission.
  B. After feeding the 5,000, Jesus refused the crowd's desire to make him king.
  C. Jesus declined to adjudicate a legitimate social justice complaint in Luke 12.

II. The biblical witness shows limited emphasis on political engagement.
  A. The apostles devoted little space to addressing political reforms in their writings.
  B. God instructed the Jewish exiles to "seek the good" of the cities where they lived.
  C. Christians engage in politics as citizens of another kingdom who witness to their King.

III. Christians can also fall into the ditch of believing earthly politics don't matter.
  A. Good politics is a way of loving our neighbors.
  B. The Christian worldview has provided many political benefits to societies.
  C. We must speak clearly where the Bible speaks clearly on moral issues.

IV. Christians should follow key rules of engagement in political discussions.
  A. Maintain unity on goals even when disagreeing on methods for achieving them.
  B. Never morally equivocate or excuse sin for political advantage.
  C. Keep Jesus' name holy by representing him accurately in all political engagement.

NOTES

DISCUSS [35 MINUTES]

Discuss what you just watched by answering the following questions.

1. Ask someone to read Mark 1:1 and 1:14–15. In light of what you have learned about the political implications of terms like *gospel* and statements such as "Jesus is Lord" in the first century, how might the original listeners have understood Christ's message? How does this impact your understanding of the kingdom of God?

2. There are two "ditches" that Christians can fall into regarding politics: (1) making earthly politics too important, or (2) acting as if they don't matter at all. Which ditch do you find yourself (or your Christian community) more prone to fall into? Why?

3. Invite someone to read Jeremiah 29:4–7. Remember that God instructed the Jewish exiles to "seek the peace and prosperity of the city" where they lived. What does this suggest about how Christians should engage politically today? How can we balance this civic responsibility with our primary identity as disciple-makers and witnesses for Christ?

4. Included among Jesus' twelve disciples were a tax collector (Matthew) and a zealot (Simon)—two men who would have had opposing political views. What do you learn from Jesus in his willingness to bring these two men together to advance his mission?

5. Christians can be united on goals even if they disagree on the best means for accomplishing them. What is an example of a goal that Christians generally agree on but might disagree about how to achieve? Have you seen these disagreements affect Christian unity? If so, what might help you to maintain unity while still engaging in these conversations?

RESPOND [10 MINUTES]

As a follower of Jesus, you are called to engage wisely in the political realm while maintaining your primary identity as a citizen of God's kingdom and witness to Jesus. Reflect on this truth as you read the following passages and answer the questions that follow.

> The kingdom of the world has become the kingdom of our Lord and of his Messiah, and he will reign for ever and ever.
>
> **REVELATION 11:15**
>
> But our citizenship is in heaven. And we eagerly await a Savior from there, the Lord Jesus Christ.
>
> **PHILIPPIANS 3:20**

How does your primary citizenship in heaven shape your engagement with earthly politics? In what ways might your political engagement change if you consistently viewed yourself first as a witness to Jesus?

Think about a recent political conversation or social media interaction you've had. How well did you represent Jesus in that moment? Did you speak with both grace and truth? What might you do differently in future political discussions?

PRAY [10 MINUTES]

As you close today, pray for wisdom in your political engagement. Ask God to help you avoid both ditches in which Christians often fall—neither *overvaluing* nor *undervaluing* earthly politics. Pray that you would speak clearly on moral issues where the Bible speaks clearly. Ask for discernment to recognize when you are being tempted to compromise your witness for political advantage. Above all, pray that your political engagement would consistently honor Jesus' name and give others an accurate picture of his character and kingdom.

Personal Study

It's common for Christians to put too much focus on politics or ignore it completely. How do you avoid either of these extremes? When you do engage in politics, how can you do it in a way that honors Jesus and draws others to him? These are tough questions—and exactly what you will be examining this week. As you work through each of these exercises, continue to write down your responses to the questions. (If you are engaging this study as part of a group, you will be given a few minutes to share your insights at the start of the next session.) If you are reading *Everyday Revolutionary* alongside this study, first review chapter 7 of the book.

Jesus Preached a Political Gospel

When we hear the word *gospel*, we often think of personal salvation—a message about sin, grace, and eternal life. But in Jesus' time, *gospel* was a political term used by Roman emperors to proclaim their accomplishments. When the messengers of an emperor announced "good news," they weren't talking about spiritual renewal. They were declaring the emperor had secured victory, expanded his empire, and brought peace through his rule.

Against this backdrop, the early Christians made a radical claim: The "good news" is that *Jesus* is Lord. This wasn't just a personal religious conviction. It was a direct challenge to Rome's authority. The true King, they insisted, wasn't seated on a Roman throne but had been born in a manger, crucified as a criminal, and raised to reign over all creation.

This reality transforms how we engage in politics. As we participate in civic life, we do so as citizens of a greater kingdom. No party, policy, or leader can claim our ultimate allegiance because we serve a higher King. This dual citizenship shapes our posture and priorities.

It also keeps us from two dangerous extremes. One is *political idolatry*—treating earthly power as if it holds the key to human flourishing. The other is *political disengagement*—retreating into isolation as if what happens here doesn't matter. Jesus calls us to a better way. We are to seek justice, advocate for the vulnerable, and work for the good of our communities, all the while recognizing that no government can bring the salvation humanity needs.

Like the early church, we are to be politically engaged but never politically enslaved. Our faith should shape our politics, but our politics must never shape our faith. Our allegiance is to a King who rules not by coercion but by love . . . not by dominance but by sacrifice.

This means we can approach political engagement with both conviction and humility—*conviction* about God's justice, but *humility* about human solutions. It means we can stand firm in truth while showing grace to those who disagree with us. It means we can work for the common good while never mistaking earthly victories for eternal ones.

One day, every ruler, nation, and system of power will bow before the rightful King. Until then, we live as citizens of two kingdoms—never forgetting which one will last forever.

Read | 1 Timothy 2:1–4; Luke 2:8–12; Matthew 10:40–42

1. In 1 Timothy 2:2, Paul tells his younger coworker that it is good to "live peaceful and quiet lives." Paul says this pleases God because he wants "all people to be saved and come to a knowledge of the truth" (verse 4). What is the connection between living peaceful and quiet lives and helping others come to know the truth about Jesus?

2. Would the non-Christians who know you (and read your social media posts) say that you live a peaceful and quiet life? Why or why not?

Caesar Augustus promised many of the things that only Jesus can bring: salvation, peace, a kingdom, heaven on earth, and happiness. Augustus dubbed his reign the *Pax Romana* (the "peace of Rome"), ushering in a new and—he believed—permanent era of peace and prosperity. But, the Gospel writers say, in a remote corner of that subjugated empire, angels declared the birth of a new King, a rival one: "Today in the town of David a Savior has been born to you; he is the Messiah, the Lord" (Luke 2:11). A Savior who was *better* than Caesar. The real Son of God, the actual Prince of Peace, the legitimate King of Kings and Lord of Lords. The Christian confession is that *Jesus* is Lord—not Caesar. Getting this right will keep us from errors in our political engagement strategy.[17]

3. The shepherds received news from the angels that not only transformed their lives but also their whole community (see Luke 2:8–12). What are some needs in your community that you could meet that would bring "great joy" to the people who live there? How might meeting those needs open doors to share the hope of Jesus?

Needs in your community	How meeting would open doors

4. How might your political engagement change if you viewed it through the lens of dual citizenship—that you are a citizen first of heaven and then of the earth?

The bottom line is that we can't pull back from politics, grieving its sliminess and saying things like, "Politics don't matter. Jesus is my President." That is precisely the opposite of what our true "President" commissioned us to do. "Seek the peace and prosperity of [your] city," he said (Jeremiah 29:7). Make its problems your problems. Get involved. This means speaking out against the sources of injustice. It means bringing God's *shalom* to every corner of Babylon—its economics, education structures, and foreign policy.[18]

5. Jesus said that even giving "a cup of cold water" in his name has eternal significance (Matthew 10:42). He doesn't call us to pull back from society but to show up with compassion and justice. Given this truth, what tangible act of kindness could you offer this week that might deeply impact someone in need?

Engage in Earthly Politics

In the middle of a storm, a seasoned sailor knows that navigating the waters requires more than just wind in the sails. It's about knowing when to steer into the waves and when to adjust course, trusting the compass while reading the shifting tides. This is a fitting image for the way Christians should navigate political involvement in a world that often feels like a turbulent sea.

It is true that "our citizenship is in heaven" (Philippians 3:20). But for now, we are anchored on this earth. Our true home is not of this world, but we are still called to engage with it wisely and faithfully. Just as a sailor navigates a storm by trusting in his compass, so we navigate this world by trusting that God has placed us where he wants us to be.

Political involvement is part of loving our neighbors, working for justice, and flourishing in our communities. But we must be cautious. Our approach to politics cannot mirror that of the world! We are not called to place our ultimate hope in earthly leaders or policies. Our hope is rooted in a kingdom that transcends all governments. While we engage in politics, we must remember that no earthly solution can bring the kingdom of God. Only Christ can do that.

In our engagement, we must balance conviction with humility. We must speak boldly where the Bible speaks clearly—advocating for truth, justice, and righteousness. Yet, at the same time, we must acknowledge that many political issues require wisdom and thoughtful application of biblical principles. Other Christians may disagree on the specifics, and that's okay.

The key is staying true to our mission. Our political involvement should never overshadow our primary calling to witness to Christ's lordship. Just as the sailor focuses on the horizon, knowing the storm will pass, so we keep our eyes on the kingdom of God. Our political participation always reflects our allegiance to Christ—not the other way around.

Navigating this dual citizenship requires wisdom and discernment. It means studying both Scripture and the political issues that affect our communities.

Is also means having the wisdom to know we work not for power or personal gain but to reflect the character of our King—especially in how we love our neighbors and care for the most vulnerable.

Read | Matthew 22:15–21; Romans 13:1–7; 1 Peter 2:13–17

1. Jesus said, "Give back to Caesar what is Caesar's, and to God what is God's" (see Matthew 22:15–21). What responsibilities do you believe you owe to the government and what belongs solely to God? Where might those areas come into conflict in your life?

2. Paul wrote that believers should "be subject to the governing authorities" who have been "established by God" (Romans 13:1), even though he lived under Nero—a ruler hostile to Christians. How does this challenge your attitude toward leaders you disagree with? Is there a specific shift in posture, tone, or behavior that God might be calling you to make?

Politics almost always involves choosing the lesser of two evils, but we must never equivocate about evil as we do so. Remember, our *ultimate* goal is not getting someone elected but presenting Christ faithfully. This means we must always come down on his side OF EVERYTHING. Clearly and unequivocally. Whether it's politically helpful or not. We're not solving for political power; we're solving for testimony. We will inevitably end up at times having to choose between imperfect options. In those situations, we simply have to vote according to our conscience. Yet we must be clear through it all, to ourselves and everybody else, about where our ultimate allegiance lies.[19]

3. Reflect on your most recent political conversations or social media posts. Would an observer clearly see your ultimate allegiance is to Christ rather than to a party or candidate? Explain your response.

4. Peter calls believers to "live as free people" while using their freedom as God's servants (1 Peter 2:16). How might your political involvement change if you approached it primarily as a servant of God rather than as simply exercising your rights as a citizen? What specific political issue might you engage with differently?

Before you imply "thus says the Lord," you should have a clear chapter-and-verse reference where "thus says the Lord." Be aware when you've crossed the line separating a clear biblical principle and an application of biblical wisdom. Of course, the goal of Christian maturity is learning to apply biblical principles in places where a biblical directive is not spelled out. So, by all means, form these secondary convictions. If you're a church leader, encourage your people to do so and equip them with the tools. But as you form these secondary convictions, live with the humility that your wisdom can be flawed and that some applications of Christian principles can change from context to context. Unless what you're saying has clear biblical support, refrain (in most cases) from attaching God's name or the church's reputation to it. Allow room for disagreement so that those who oppose you aren't seen as the enemies of God.[20]

5. Consider a political position you hold strongly. Can you identify which aspects are clearly biblical and which are formed from your secondary convictions? How might this distinction affect how you discuss this issue?

> Which aspects are clearly biblical . . .

> Which are formed from your secondary convictions . . .

> How this disctinction might affect how you discuss this issue . . .

Speak Where the Bible Speaks

Imagine you're driving on a winding mountain road. Some parts are clearly marked with solid lines, indicating there are hazards and you shouldn't pass. Other parts are marked with dotted lines, signaling areas where caution is needed in passing. As drivers, we know to follow the solid lines with absolute certainty and approach the dotted lines with careful discernment.

Christians are called to navigate life in much the same way—to distinguish between unshakable truths and areas where we must apply wisdom. In today's world, it can be easy to confuse the two. Some of us approach issues with a "solid line" mentality, making every matter an absolute statement of faith. Others of us take the opposite approach, treating all matters as open for interpretation, afraid of stepping on any toes. Both extremes miss the mark.

The Bible provides us with solid *and* dotted lines. Solid lines represent core truths—God's design for life, the sanctity of marriage, the inherent value of all people, and our call to protect the vulnerable. These are nonnegotiable truths that shape our faith and actions. Dotted lines represent areas where Scripture offers guidance but the application may vary depending on context. These areas require careful thought, prayer, and humility.

The challenge lies in discerning when to speak with certainty and when to allow for different perspectives. We must speak with clarity on the truths the Bible makes absolutely clear. For example, Peter's statement that "salvation is to be found through [Jesus] alone" (Acts 4:12 GNT) is an absolute truth we must defend and proclaim. However, Paul's comment "Now to the unmarried and the widows I say: It is good for them to stay unmarried, as I do" (1 Corinthians 7:8) is an example of practice advice (as Paul himself admits).

Our words, whether solid-line absolutes or dotted-line guidance, should *always* point others to Christ. The aim is not to win arguments or prove ourselves right but to draw people into relationship with Jesus. This approach requires both boldness and grace. We must be bold in standing firm on truths . . .

but exhibit grace in conversations where opinions differ. This balance is especially crucial in everyday interactions—at work, with family, and online—for each and every conversation offers an opportunity to point others to the gospel.

Read | Acts 20:26–27; Ephesians 4:14–15; Proverbs 31:8–9

1. In Paul's farewell address to the Ephesian elders, he says, "I am innocent of the blood of any of you. For I have not hesitated to proclaim to you the whole will of God" (Acts 20:26–27). What did Paul mean when he said he had proclaimed "the whole will of God"? What does it mean in your life to proclaim "the whole will of God"?

2. Paul calls us to speak the truth to others in love (see Ephesians 4:14–15). Which way do you tend to lean—being truthful but lacking love or being loving while avoiding hard truths? What are some problems that leaning too far one way or the other can cause?

Even "truth speaking" must be done under the master assignment of being a faithful witness, which means not only being concerned with rebuking a wayward culture but also being concerned with what people think about Jesus. That means we take *extra* precautions to make sure we distance ourselves from any "evil" that people associate with us politically. Our *primary* concern in all things is that people think rightly about Christ. His is the only name under heaven by which we can be saved, and we've got to keep the path to Jesus clear of unnecessary obstacles. We set him apart as holy.[21]

3. It is important to "keep the path to Jesus clear of unnecessary obstacles." Do you tend to focus more on rebuking culture than on revealing Christ? If so, what could you do to more *intentionally* point people to Jesus in your conversations and social interactions?

4. Proverbs 31:8–9 calls us to "speak up for those who cannot speak for themselves" and "defend the rights of the poor and needy." Why do you think justice and advocacy matter so deeply to God? Considering your unique position, abilities, and resources, how might God be equipping you to stand up for others in ways others may not be able to?

5. What are some of the fears you have when it comes to actually speaking out against what God says is sin? In what areas would you like to receive greater boldness from God?

> Fears you have when it comes to speaking out against sin . . .

> Areas in which you would like to receive greater boldness from God . . .

We are responsible to testify to the whole counsel of God. We do that even if it means we end up in a lion's den. We're not only solving for a better nation; we're solving for a clear testimony to Jesus. If we are associated with an evil and we don't speak out clearly against it, we tarnish the name of Jesus. When we stay quiet in the face of injustice for fear that it damages our political preferences, we show that we are more caught up in the politics of Caesar than we are the commission of heaven. Our silence in the face of celebrated wickedness makes it hard for unbelieving people on the other side to really comprehend the glory of Jesus. Our vote in each election matters, but our witness to Christ's kingdom matters more. *Christ's name must be kept holy.*[22]

Connect and Discuss

Take some time today to connect with a fellow group member and discuss some of the key insights from this session. Use any of the following prompts to help guide your discussion.

What did you like best from the content in this session, including both the group study and personal study? Why?

Do you tend to be the too-into-politics type or the avoid-politics-at-all-costs type? Did this session lead you to reconsider your position?

What was the best thing you discovered this week about how to engage in politics in a God-honoring way?

Do you tend to lean more heavily on handing out truth or giving grace? What would help you to have more balance?

What do you feel most excited to explore in the sessions ahead? Why?

Catch Up and Read Ahead

Use this time to go back and complete any of the study and reflection questions from previous days that you weren't able to finish. Make a note below of any revelations you've had and reflect on any growth or personal insights you've gained.

Read chapters 8–9 in *Everyday Revolutionary* before the next group gathering. Use the space below to make note of anything in those chapters that stands out to you or encourages you.

| **BEFORE GROUP MEETING** | Read chapters 8–9 in *Everyday Revolutionary*
 Read the Welcome section (page 68) |

| **GROUP MEETING** | Discuss the Connect questions
 Watch the video teaching for session 4
 Discuss the questions that follow as a group
 Do the closing exercise and pray (pages 68–72) |

STUDY 1	Complete the personal study (pages 74–79)
STUDY 2	Complete the personal study (pages 80–83)
STUDY 3	Complete the personal study (pages 84–87)

| **CONNECT AND DISCUSS** | Connect with one or two group members
 Discuss the follow-up questions (page 88) |

| **CATCH UP AND READ AHEAD**
 (BEFORE WEEK 5 GROUP MEETING) | Read chapters 10–12 in *Everyday Revolutionary*
 Complete any unfinished personal studies
 (page 89) |

Live Quietly:

Creation-Fulfilling and Excellence-Pursuing

Whatever you do, do it all for the glory of God.

1 CORINTHIANS 10:31

WELCOME [READ ON YOUR OWN]

The renowned British writer Dorothy Sayers observed a profound disconnect in how Christians viewed their work. In a 1942 essay, she wrote, "In nothing has the Church so lost her hold on reality as in her failure to understand and respect the secular vocation. She has allowed work and religion to become separate departments."[23]

Sayers challenged the notion that only religious vocations have spiritual significance. She argued that medieval cathedral builders didn't divide their efforts into "sacred" and "secular" portions. They simply brought excellent craftsmanship to every aspect of their work—from visible spires to hidden stone carvings that only God would see.

"The Church's approach to an intelligent carpenter," she continued, "is usually confined to exhorting him not to be drunk and disorderly in his leisure hours, and to come to church on Sundays. What the Church should be telling him is this: that the very first demand that his religion makes upon him is that he should make good tables."[24]

For Sayers, good craftsmanship was a means to evangelism and a form of worship—an offering that honored the Creator. "The only Christian work is good work well done," she insisted. "Work is not, primarily, a thing one does to live, but the thing one lives to do."[25]

Sayers's perspective echoes what Christians throughout history have discovered. Our daily work, when done with excellence and integrity, can be a powerful witness for Christ. The engineer designing safe bridges, the teacher preparing thorough lessons, the builder going a step beyond in constructing a house—all participate in God's creative work and testify to his character through their craftsmanship.

CONNECT [10 MINUTES]

Get the session started by choosing one or both of the following questions to discuss together as a group.

- What is something that spoke to you in last week's personal study that you would like to share with the group?

— *or* —

- As a child, what did you want to be when you "grew up"? How does that compare with what you do now?

WATCH [25 MINUTES]

Now watch the video for this session. Below is an outline of the main points covered during the teaching. Record any key concepts that stand out to you.

OUTLINE

I. Christians often misunderstand what it means to be a witness in their everyday lives.

   A. Many Christians today confuse their witness with overt evangelistic displays or religious branding.

   B. The apostles advocated for living "quietly" as an important aspect of witness.

   C. Paul instructed believers to "aspire to live quietly" and "mind your own affairs."

   D. Peter encouraged Christians to live "good" (beautiful/remarkable) lives among non-believers.

II. Living quietly creates opportunities for more explicit testimony.

   A. The apostles certainly engaged in bold, public proclamation of the gospel.

   B. Yet they saw quiet, beautiful living as creating credibility for these moments.

   C. Peter notes that "living beautifully" prompts non-believers to ask about our hope.

   D. Two practices can help us live as everyday revolutionaries in any context.

III. First practice: Creation-fulfilling work honors our design as image-bearers.

   A. Like Eric Liddell in *Chariots of Fire*, we can "feel God's pleasure" in our work.

   B. The Creation Mandate preceded the Great Commission as God's first assignment to humans.

   C. Work is not a punishment but participation in God's ongoing creative activity.

   D. The Holy Spirit empowers both sacred and secular vocations (like Bezalel's craftsmanship).

IV. Second practice: Excellence-pursuing work honors God's reputation.

   A. Paul instructed believers to do everything "in the name of the Lord Jesus."

   B. Daniel was found to be "ten times" better than others in Nebuchadnezzar's court.

   C. Daniel's excellence was characterized by being neither corrupt nor negligent.

   D. Our work becomes an offering to God that represents his character to others.

NOTES

DISCUSS [35 MINUTES]

Discuss what you just watched by answering the following questions.

1. Invite someone in the group to read aloud Exodus 31:1–5. In this passage, the Holy Spirit empowers Bezalel's artistic abilities. What does that tell you about God's perspective on work? How should this impact your view of spiritual gifts?

2. Ask someone to read aloud Daniel 6:3–4. How is Daniel's work described in this passage? In what ways did that reflect on the God whom he served?

3. Now read Colossians 3:17. What does it mean to do your work "in the name of the Lord Jesus"? How might this perspective transform how you view mundane tasks?

4. Both our creation-fulfilling work and our excellence-pursuing work prepare the soil for evangelism. What is an example of a time when someone's creative or excellent work gave you an opportunity to engage in a spiritual conversation with another person?

5. Daniel's excellent work in Babylon earned him influence and opened doors for him to speak truth to power. What are some of the ways that *your* excellent work might earn you similar opportunities within your own Babylonian contexts?

RESPOND [10 MINUTES]

As a follower of Jesus, you are called to engage wisely in the political realm while maintaining your primary identity as a citizen of God's kingdom and witness to Jesus. Reflect on these facts as you read the following passages and answer the questions.

> Aspire to live quietly, and to mind your own affairs, and to work with your hands, as we instructed you.
>
> **1 THESSALONIANS 4:11** ESV

> Whatever you do, work at it with all your heart, as working for the Lord, not for human masters, since you know that you will receive an inheritance from the Lord as a reward. It is the Lord Christ you are serving.
>
> **COLOSSIANS 3:23-24**

In what aspects of your work (paid or unpaid) do you clearly feel God's pleasure? How can you embrace these aspects as participanting in God's ongoing greater work?

Consider the quality of your work. If Jesus were to evaluate it as an offering to him, what areas might need improvement? What would it look like to pursue excellence in those areas not primarily for career advancement or recognition but as a witness to his character?

PRAY [10 MINUTES]

As you close this session, thank God for the privilege of participating in his ongoing creative work through your daily vocation. Ask him to help you see your work—whether in an office, classroom, home, or elsewhere—as a sacred calling and an opportunity to share about Christ. Pray for the courage and discipline to pursue excellence not for personal gain but as an offering that honors Jesus' name. Ask for wisdom to discern how your quiet witness of remarkable work might create opportunities to speak about the hope that is within you.

Personal Study

We live in a world that tends to be loud. People shout their opinions and use ALL CAPS in their social media posts. Yet it is in this loud, polarized, opinionated world that God tells us to "aspire to live quietly, and to mind your own affairs" (1 Thessalonians 4:11 ESV). But how do we do that? If we do, will we lose our influence? Or is it possible a distinctively quiet witness is *exactly* what is needed in this loud world? This week, you were introduced to the first two of five ways that you can live quietly for Jesus, which you will continue to explore in this personal study. As you work through each of these exercises, be sure to keep writing down your responses to the questions. (Again, if you are engaging this study as part of a group, you will be given a few minutes to share your insights at the start of the next session.) If you are reading *Everyday Revolutionary* alongside this study, first review chapters 8–9 of the book.

STUDY 1

Quietly Living

It's fascinating to watch professional photographers at work. When it comes to their craft, it's not about chasing the loudest moments but about patiently waiting for the right shot. In other words, the key to their success as photographers is not about forcing dramatic scenes but about capturing authentic moments with excellence.

This quiet approach offers a metaphor for how we influence our communities. In a culture that celebrates grand gestures, our lasting influence comes from consistent presence. We don't need to shout to be heard. We just need to live in such a way that our presence is unmistakable, our character undeniable, and our faith in Christ a subtle force for good.

Think about how light transforms a room. It doesn't announce itself. It just fills the space . . . revealing beauty, exposing what needs attention, and creating warmth. The influence of light is quiet yet transformative. Our lives can illuminate our surroundings in the same way.

Consider a time when someone's quiet influence impacted you. Maybe it was a colleague who made every meeting more productive with her calm demeanor. Or a neighbor whose small acts of kindness reshaped the atmosphere. Or a parent who approached the daily, mundane, repetitive tasks of caring for a child with grace. These people didn't demand attention. They just lived their faith in ways that changed the environment.

This is what it means to live as light in the world. In photography terms, you're creating "depth of field"—keeping every area of your life in focus from work to relationships. You're paying attention to the "composition"—how your life reflects God's character. You're mastering the "exposure"—allowing your faith to shine through naturally. This quiet living requires both skill and awareness. Like a photographer who knows both the science and the art of light, you combine competence with character in ways that point to the source of your light.

So, today, think about one area where you can show up with excellence. Respond with patience. Offer encouragement. Simply reflect God's light in your actions. When you live out your faith quietly and consistently in this way, you will transform the world around you.

Read | 1 Thessalonians 4:9–12; Romans 12:17–19; 1 Peter 2:11–12

1. In 1 Thessalonians 4:9–12, Paul gives instructions about how to live quietly. In the chart below, read each of the items that Paul lists and then write down: (1) how you are currently doing in that area, and (2) what steps you could take to improve.

Verse	How you are currently doing in this area
"Love . . . one another" (verse 9)	
"Mind your own business" (verse 11)	
"Work with your hands" (verse 11)	
"Win the respect of outsiders" (verse 12)	
"Not be dependent on anybody" (verse 12)	

Verse	What steps you could take to improve
"Love . . . one another" (verse 9)	
"Mind your own business" (verse 11)	
"Work with your hands" (verse 11)	
"Win the respect of outsiders" (verse 12)	
"Not be dependent on anybody" (verse 12)	

2. In Romans 12:17–19, Paul presents a challenging call: hold firmly to truth ("do what is right in the eyes of everyone") while also pursuing peace ("do not take revenge"). Can you think of a situation in which you find it difficult to do both? What would be necessary in that situation for you to stand by your convictions while also seeking to live at peace?

Both Peter and Paul give us a "keep your head down and do your job" vibe. But don't they want us to loudly proclaim the gospel? Wasn't Peter the stand-up-and-give-a-sermon-in-the-temple-square-and-3,000-people-get-saved guy? Didn't Paul once preach before an amphitheater filled with angry Ephesians? Yes, both loudly testified to the gospel, and both lost their lives for doing so. And yet both told early Christians to pursue the quiet life, because it would be the quietness of their everyday lives that would create opportunities for, and give credence to, their moments of loud testimony. The beauty found in their quietness of life would be so compelling, in fact, that Peter anticipated it would drive Babylonians to *ask* the reason for the hope that drove them.[26]

3. Peter tells us the quietness of our everyday lives leads to beauty, which leads people to ask questions, which leads to open doors to share the gospel (see 1 Peter 2:11–12):

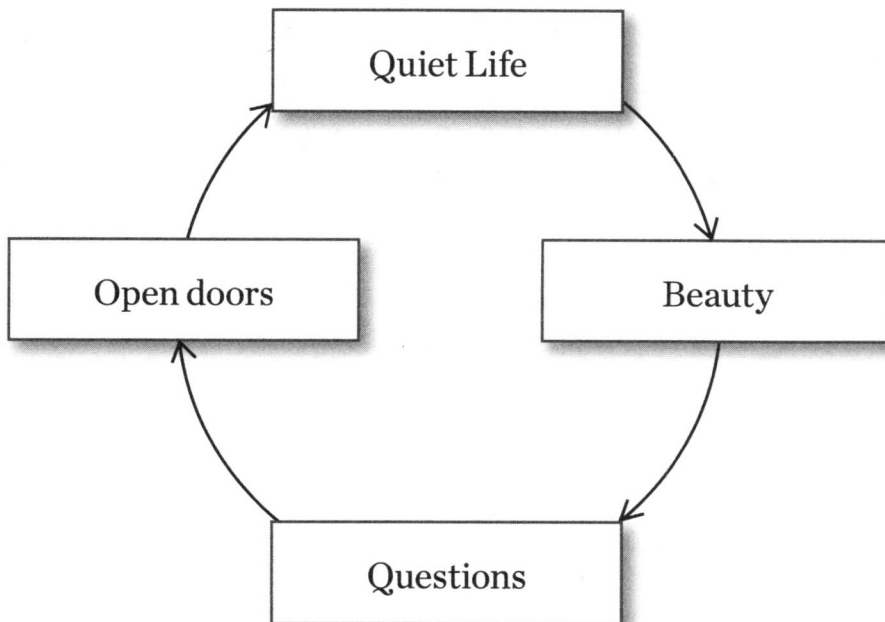

Quiet Life → Beauty → Questions → Open doors → Quiet Life

What is "beautiful" about your life? What questions might it lead people to ask?

What response would you give if people asked you about the way you live? How could this present you with open doors to share about the gospel?

4. Now think about your work ethic, your attitude about your job, how you treat others, and the quality of your work. How could excellence in those areas point others to Jesus?

For years, I viewed secular jobs as second class in God's kingdom—a kind of means-to-an-end for funding *real* kingdom work. Real kingdom work, I assumed, happens from pulpits, choir lofts, and writer's desks. The rest of our secular jobs are necessary evils to pay the bills, but for *true* Christians, their life's passion is *church work*. But being a full-time servant of Jesus is not something we do *after* we pay the bills; it's what we do *as* we pay the bills. Cleaning up a room for others to meet in, whether that's so they can participate in an evangelistic sermon, enjoy a country music concert, or take part in a job fair, is a way of serving God by fulfilling the creation commission. *The way* we do our work and the spirit we carry with us in it points people to our Creator.[27]

5. God is as concerned with displaying his power *outside* the walls of the church as he is with displaying his power *within* those walls. So, what opportunity in your workplace, neighborhood, or community life might God be inviting you to recognize as ministry? What steps could you take to be more intentional about this opportunity?

Creation-Fulfilling

You step into a studio where a masterpiece is unfolding. The artist has begun with broad strokes and vibrant colors, creating something stunning but intentionally incomplete. Then, unexpectedly, the artist hands you a brush and invites you to contribute. This isn't a beginner's art class—your contribution is part of the design, intended to enhance the piece.

This image illustrates God's unique approach to creation. When God looked at his work and called it "good" instead of "perfect" (see Genesis 1:31), he wasn't expressing limitation. He was leaving space for us to participate. We see this is true in the next part of the story: "Now the LORD God had formed out of the ground all the wild animals and all the birds in the sky. He brought them to the man to see what he would name them; and whatever the man called each living creature, that was its name" (2:19). God actually *invited* Adam to join in the creative process through giving names to each of the animals.

God chose not to work alone. He still chooses not to work alone. He invites us to share in the creative process, allowing our efforts to shape and cultivate the world around us.

What if we saw our daily work—whether it's teaching, coding, cooking, cleaning, or leading—not as just tasks to get done but as opportunities to add our unique brushstroke to God's ongoing masterpiece? The accountant organizing numbers, the mechanic fixing engines, the nurse offering care . . . all are part of God's creative work. Even the most routine or unnoticed tasks become significant when we view them through this lens.

When we work with integrity and excellence, we align ourselves with the Creator's nature, bringing order, beauty, and life from chaos. This perspective changes how we approach our work. We no longer pursue excellence just for a paycheck or recognition but because our efforts are part of a greater—and *eternal*—story that God has been writing. Each task is an act of worship and a way to reflect God's image as Creator.

And that feeling of satisfaction when our work is done well? It's a glimpse of the joy God experienced as he created. Meaning in our work comes not only from the *results* but from the *process* itself. We know that our labor, no matter how small, contributes to something eternal.

Read | Genesis 1:26–31; 2:1–3, 15–17; 3:17–18

1. God blessed Adam and Eve before giving them work to do (see Genesis 1:28). How might approaching your work from a position of *already* being blessed by God—rather than trying to earn that blessing—change your motivation or reduce your stress?

The Great Commission was not the *first* commission God gave to his people. The *first* commission God gave his people was to make the world a better place to live in—to extend the boundaries of Eden to the ends of the earth. When God placed Adam in the Garden of Eden, he didn't just tell him to keep away from a few bad apples; he commissioned Adam to develop the Garden to make it a more beautiful and habitable place to live (see Genesis 2:15). That's what the Hebrew word *abad* (which we translate as "work") implies. God gave Adam a job as his co-creator.[28]

2. God didn't rest because he was tired. No, he rested so that he could enjoy and appreciate his work (see Genesis 2:1–3). When was the last time you took time to simply appreciate what you accomplished? How would regular celebration change your approach to work?

3. God communicated directly with Adam about his purpose and boundaries (see Genesis 2:15–17). How regular is your communication with God about your work and life direction? What practice could help you ask and listen better for his guidance?

Work was not a punishment inflicted by God because of Adam and Eve's sin, as if God's original plan had been for them to just sit around all day strumming their harps and sipping on nonalcoholic piña coladas. No, God put Adam and Eve into a world with gardens that needed cultivating, buildings that needed building, art that needed painting, music that needed composing, faces that needed make-upping, supply chains that needed organizing, and justice systems that needed formulating. In this unfinished world he intends for us to be his co-creators, his regents, in helping to shape a planet beautiful in form, realized in potential, and useful for humans.[29]

4. One consequence of Adam and Eve's sin was that God "cursed the ground" and said it would "produce thorns and thistles" (Genesis 3:17–18). How might this have impacted views about work? What is the proper understanding about work in the Creation story?

5. For two millennia, Christians have referred to "thin" places where the separation between the mundane and the divine is narrow—places where the sacred is sensed in the ordinary. When have you experienced work as such a "thin" place? What in particular made it feel that way to you?

Excellence-Pursuing

Excellence isn't about being perfect but about being devoted. It's a posture of the heart that puts purpose into every task, big or small. Excellence isn't just a skill but a mindset—a choice to do what you do with reverence for God, whether in high-profile projects or ordinary moments.

Think about Daniel. He was a young Jewish man living in the foreign nation of Babylon, surrounded by a culture that mocked his faith. However, instead of compromising, he allowed his work to reflect God's character. "Daniel distinguished himself . . . because he had an extraordinary spirit" (Daniel 6:3 NEB). His excellence wasn't driven by ambition but by devotion to God. His work wasn't for the approval of men but for God alone.

This is the power of excellence. In a world that rewards shortcuts, those who persist in always giving it their best stand out. The coach who invests deeply in students. The manager who takes the time to check in daily with employees. The mechanic who takes the extra step of making sure the part just installed won't immediately fail again. These are the people who make a difference. Excellence in any field reflects God's order and beauty in a broken world.

Paul reminds us, "Whatever you do, do it from the heart, as something done for the Lord and not for people" (Colossians 3:23 CSB). When we perform our work as if we are doing it for *God*, our excellence becomes an act of worship. It becomes an offering not just to those we serve but also to the Creator who calls us to live with purpose.

True excellence isn't just about skill but about character. Are we reliable even when no one is watching? Do we seek to bring peace to every conflict? Do we respond to others with encouragement or discouragement? Excellence is faithfulness in action. It is consistently showing up with a spirit of devotion regardless of the task.

When we live this way, much like in Daniel's story, people will notice. Our commitment to doing things well becomes a quiet witness—a kind of living apologetic. It provides an invitation for others to ask, "Why don't you compromise like everyone else?" In that moment, we have the chance to point them to the source of all goodness, beauty, and truth.

So today, as you go about your work, look for how you can reflect God's glory in each task. Let your devotion be a living testimony of God's excellence. Seek to draw others through your excellence to the God who calls you to do all things with his heart and for his kingdom.

Read | Matthew 25:14–23; 25:24–30; Philippians 2:1–4

1. In the parable Jesus tells in Matthew 25:14–23, the faithful servants immediately put the money the master had given them to work. In what area of your professional life might you be hesitating to fully invest your skills, knowledge, resources, or effort? How might recognizing your abilities as God-given gifts change your approach to your job?

2. The unfaithful servant acted out of fear and then blamed his master for his own lack of initiative (see verses 24–30). How might fear be holding you back from excelling in a specific area of your work? In what professional situation might you be blaming circumstances or others rather than taking responsibility for bringing your best?

It's not just *what* work we do but *how* we do it that directs our community's attention to the worthiness of God. Living with integrity matters because we reflect the character of God. It's part of how we "shine" in Babylon. Justice is, as the psalmist tells us, the very foundation of God's throne (see Psalm 89:14). God's reputation for justice, in fact, is foundational to the world's understanding of the gospel. Shining in Babylon means never sullying his name by association with a false balance, a fudged return, or a willingness to compromise for a financial advantage.[30]

3. Your work is a testimony to Christ's nature and character. How do you see Jesus' reputation as being on the line in the following areas of your job?

Area	How Jesus' reputation is on the line
Quality of work:	
Attitude at work:	
Motivation for work:	
How you treat others:	

4. In Philippians 2:3–4, Paul stresses the importance of valuing others above yourself and placing their interests above your own. What would it look like if you consistently did this at your place of work? In what ways do you think it would stand out to others?

Do you really want to get the world's attention? Do you want to shine a light on Christ in a culture that doesn't "get" you? Then do a great job for an earthly boss who is a jerk and doesn't give you the first word of recognition. Lots of Babylonians work hard, but they do it primarily for money, promotion, and praise. Paul, however, says in Colossians 3:23–25 that it's when you work hard *without* those motivations that people will be moved to ask, "What in the world could possibly be motivating you?" To which you say, "Actually, nothing in this world motivates me. My Boss waiting in another world does."[31]

5. Perhaps you work for an earthly boss who is "a jerk" and gives you no recognition. The good news is that *God* is your true Boss. You are working for him, and your work is worship. How will you remind yourself of this truth throughout your workday?

Connect and Discuss

Take some time today to connect with a fellow group member and discuss some of the key insights from this session. Use any of the following prompts to help guide your discussion.

What did you like best from the content in this session, including both the group study and personal study? Why?

What is your "job"? What do you like and not like about it?

Did your perspective on your daily work and tasks change because of what you learned this week? If so, in what ways?

What opportunities do you have right now to love God and people through the work you do?

How could you become a more effective witness for Jesus at your work?

What do you feel most excited to explore in the sessions ahead? Why?

Catch Up and Read Ahead

Use this time to go back and complete any of the study and reflection questions from previous days that you weren't able to finish. Make a note below of any revelations you've had and reflect on any growth or personal insights you've gained.

Read chapters 10–12 in *Everyday Revolutionary* before the next group gathering. Use the space below to make note of anything in those chapters that stands out to you or encourages you.

BEFORE GROUP MEETING	Read chapters 10–12 in *Everyday Revolutionary* Read the Welcome section (page 92)
GROUP MEETING	Discuss the Connect questions Watch the video teaching for session 5 Discuss the questions that follow as a group Do the closing exercise and pray (pages 92–96)
STUDY 1	Complete the personal study (pages 98–101)
STUDY 2	Complete the personal study (pages 102–105)
STUDY 3	Complete the personal study (pages 106–109)
CONNECT AND DISCUSS	Connect with one or two group members Discuss the follow-up questions (page 110)
CATCH UP AND READ AHEAD (BEFORE WEEK 6 GROUP MEETING)	Read chapters 13–17 in *Everyday Revolutionary* Complete any unfinished personal studies (page 111)

Live Quietly:

Holiness-Reflecting, Redemption-Displaying, and Mission-Advancing

I have become all things to all people so that by all possible means I might save some. I do all this for the sake of the gospel, that I may share in its blessings.

1 CORINTHIANS 9:22-23

WELCOME [READ ON YOUR OWN]

In 1966, Dr. Paul Brand, a brilliant orthopedic surgeon, moved to southern India. Brand had become fascinated with leprosy patients and their loss of sensation. In his reasearch, he discovered something revolutionary: Leprosy itself didn't directly cause the disfigurement associated with the disease; rather, it was the loss of pain sensation that allowed patients to unknowingly damage their own extremities.

In the caste system in India where leprosy patients were considered among the "untouchables"—the lowest rung of society—Brand's approach was radical. He touched them. He interacted with them. He developed surgical techniques to prevent and repair damage to their hands and feet. His corrective tendon transfer surgeries restored functionality to thousands of patients' hands, allowing them to work, feed themselves, and rejoin society.

Brand's surgical excellence opened doors that would have remained closed to traditional missionary approaches. Government officials who were suspicious of Christians welcomed his medical expertise. Where other foreigners faced restrictions, Brand received invitations to train surgeons throughout India and eventually worldwide.[32]

Brand's approach to medicine fundamentally changed how the world understood and treated leprosy. When he was asked about the source of his compassion and commitment to excellence, he would speak openly about his faith in Christ. As he wrote in his memoir, "In my work with people who have leprosy, I often think of Jesus' dealings with leprosy. He was unafraid. He touched those whom no one else would touch."[33]

The life of Dr. Brand demonstrates how excellence coupled with compassion can create natural opportunities for us to share Jesus. Our quiet excellence will speak more loudly than words alone, embodying the final three qualities we will explore in this session: holiness-reflecting integrity, redemption-displaying grace, and mission-advancing purpose.

CONNECT [10 MINUTES]

Get the session started by choosing one or both of the following questions to discuss together as a group.

- What is something that spoke to you in last week's personal study that you would like to share with the group?

— *or* —

- When has your expertise in a certain area given you the opportunity to not only help others but also represent the character of Jesus to them?

WATCH [25 MINUTES]

Now watch the video for this session. Below is an outline of the main points covered during the teaching. Record any key concepts that stand out to you.

OUTLINE

I. The "quiet life" is the starting point for effective witness in a post-Christian context.
   A. The practices of creation-fulfilling and excellence-pursuing, which we explored in the previous session, set the stage for us to share our testimony.
   B. Three additional objectives will complete our understanding of living quietly yet powerfully.
   C. Together, these five practices help us to fulfill our purpose in our Babylon.

II. Third practice: Holiness-reflecting work demonstrates God's character.
   A. Paul instructed believers to do everything "in the name of the Lord Jesus."
   B. Our work must maintain the highest levels of integrity to represent God accurately.
   C. Bosses and employees alike answer ultimately to their Master in heaven.
   D. Daniel's reputation for being neither corrupt nor negligent reflected on his God.

III. Fourth practice: Redemption-displaying interactions demonstrate God's grace.
   A. Those who have received great grace become distributors of grace to others.
   B. The story of Jean Valjean in the story *Les Misérables* illustrates the transforming power of grace.
   C. Christians develop an instinct for grace even in competitive workplace environments.
   D. Showing unexpected kindness creates opportunities to explain the Source of our generosity.

IV. Fifth practice: Mission-advancing work fulfills our primary purpose.
   A. All Christians are called to ministry as part of their mission to follow Jesus.
   B. The workplace provides access to people who may never enter a church.
   C. "Do you see a man skillful in his work? He will stand before kings" (Proverbs 22:29 ESV).
   D. God has sovereignly placed us in our careers to advance his mission.

NOTES

DISCUSS [35 MINUTES]

Discuss what you just watched by answering the following questions.

1. Of the five practices discussed on how to "live quietly" before others (creation-fulfilling, excellence-pursuing, holiness-reflecting, redemption-displaying, mission-advancing), which most challenges your current approach to your work or daily activities? Why?

2. Demonstrating integrity—whether that is at work, at school, in the home, or anywhere else—reflects positively on God's character. In what area of your life do you see the greatest potential to "stand out" because of your integrity? Why?

3. Ask someone to read Proverbs 11:1. Why does God consider dishonest business practices an "abomination"? How does this shape your understanding of marketplace ethics?

4. Invite someone to read Matthew 4:18–19. Notice that Jesus included a call for *ministry*—"to fish for people"—in his call for Peter and Andrew to become his disciples. What does this say about what Jesus expects from you when you become his disciple? How should this understanding of "ministry" impact how you view our daily work?

5. God has actually arranged where you live and where you work for the purpose of his mission. As you consider this truth, what might be some of the reasons as to why he has led you to live where you live or work where you work?

RESPOND [10 MINUTES]

As followers of Jesus, the way we live can be a powerful testimony to others. We can reflect God's holiness, display Christ's redemption, and advance the Lord's mission simply through the example we set for others. Take a few minutes on your own to reflect on these truths as you read the following passages and then answer the questions.

> Do you see someone skilled in their work? They will serve before kings; they will not serve before officials of low rank.
>
> **PROVERBS 22:29**

> And he has committed to us the message of reconciliation. We are therefore Christ's ambassadors, as though God were making his appeal through us. We implore you on Christ's behalf: Be reconciled to God.
>
> **2 CORINTHIANS 5:19-20**

Based on the holiness-reflecting objective, what is one area in your work where maintaining integrity might be challenging but would honor God's character? What steps could you take to ensure your conduct in this area reflects well on Christ?

Consider the mission-advancing objective. What relationships in your workplace, school, or community represent open doors for you to share Jesus? What are some ways you could serve as "Christ's ambassador" in that particular relationship?

PRAY [10 MINUTES]

As you end your group time, pray that God would help you integrate all five quiet-living practices into your work and relationships. Ask for discernment to maintain the highest integrity in challenging situations. Pray for opportunities to demonstrate God's unexpected grace to others and for the wisdom to recognize the mission opportunities the Lord has placed before you. Ask that your life would become compelling evidence of the transforming power of the gospel and would create natural opportunities to share the reason for your hope.

Personal Study

Last week, you began thinking about God's calling to live quietly and how that can be a powerful witness in an often-too-loud world. This week, you will continue by considering the three ways to live quietly presented in this session: holiness-reflecting, redemption-displaying, and mission-advancing. Continue to write down your insights and reflections as you work through these exercises. (If you are engaging this study as part of a group, you will again be given a few minutes to share your insights at the next session.) If you are reading *Everyday Revolutionary* alongside this study, first review chapters 10–12 of the book.

Holiness-Reflecting

Step into the kitchen of a world-class restaurant and you'll find more than just the scent of sizzling ingredients. You will also witness *precision, order,* and *discipline.* Chefs follow a principle called *mise en place,* or "everything in its place." Before any cooking begins, the ingredients are measured, tools arranged, and workspaces made pristine.

This discipline isn't just about efficiency. It is a mindset adopted by world-class cooks. It reflects a belief that the process matters as much as the final dish. In the same way, the "holiness" we display in our work isn't just about avoiding ethical violations but about how we reflect God's character in every moment. Just as a great chef's commitment to excellence shapes every step of preparation, so our pursuit of holiness permeates every detail of our work. It's not just about doing the right thing when it's easy but about cultivating faithfulness, diligence, and integrity in the small choices that shape who we are.

Consider how this plays out each day. When contractors choose solid craftsmanship over shortcuts, even though cheaper materials would pass inspection, they embody God's commitment to truth. When managers ensure fair pay despite industry pressure to cut costs, they reflect God's justice. When teachers stay after hours to coach a struggling student, even when exhaustion begs them to go home, they mirror God's compassion.

These choices, though often unnoticed, create a ripple effect. They shape workplace cultures, influence others, and point to a higher standard. But holiness isn't just about individual actions—it extends to the environments we create. Do our workplaces foster dignity or diminish it? Do our business practices promote flourishing or exploitation? Even the tone we set—whether one of grace or hostility—reveals something about the God we serve.

Of course, this commitment to holiness often comes at a cost. Like Daniel, we may face pressure to compromise or to accept *that's just how business works* as an excuse for cutting corners. But true holiness stands firm even when there is a price to be paid.

This is precisely what makes it powerful. When we consistently choose integrity over expediency, fairness over advantage, and service over self-interest, it creates a contrast from the world. It makes people stop and wonder. And when they ask why we live and work this way, we get to point them to the One whose holiness transforms everything.

Read | Psalm 15:1–5; Luke 16:10–12; Colossians 3:12–17

1. In Psalm 15:1–5, we see how much God cares about us living holy lives of integrity. The psalmist essentially asks, "Who may live in God's presence? What is required of such an individual?" How does the psalmist answer this question? What are some of the traits he identifies that would help you to likewise lead a holy life of integrity?

2. Jesus taught that those who are faithful with little can be trusted with much (see Luke 16:10–12). If you are asking God for "more"—whether that is more responsibility, influence, or resources—how might he be inviting you to demonstrate faithfulness with what you already have? What specific area could you steward more intentionally?

I have a friend who built skyscrapers in Chicago. He said it was customary for the big players in the industry to withhold the last payment to contractors as a way of manipulating them into taking new jobs with them at discounted rates. It's unfair, but these central players are so big that contractors have no choice but to do it. My friend (who represented one of these big players) said that for him, as a Christian, that presented a dilemma. Paying fairly disadvantaged him, at least in the short run, because it forfeited his leverage with contractors. And yet, he said, it didn't feel right to unfairly withhold payment if the name of the Lord Jesus was attached to his work. Our conduct in Babylon should not only be excellent but also make plain that we serve a God of justice and fairness. Our work, if done in his name, should reflect not only his excellence, but his holiness.[34]

3. In your line of work, or in your field of study, are there common practices that likewise create tension between "business as usual" and living out your Christian values? How do you navigate those tensions in a way that makes Jesus look good?

4. Paul lists several virtues in Colossians 3:12–17 that you should "clothe yourselves with" as a way to reflect God's holiness. Circle the virtue below that you feel you are the *best* at displaying in your life. Put a square around the virtue that is most *challenging* for you.

Compassion   Kindness   Humility

Gentleness   Patience   Forgiveness

What is one practical step you could take this week to grow in that area?

> I sometimes find myself wanting to quote George Whitefield in my sermons or share a profound insight I've learned from his life. But usually I don't—or at least, when I do, I keep his name out of it. That's tragic, because there is so much I'd love our church to learn from George Whitefield. But you see, there's an African American woman on our church staff from south Georgia whose family traces their lineage directly back to George Whitefield's plantations. Her ancestors remained enslaved, in part, because Whitefield compromised, and it doesn't feel right for me to publicly celebrate a man whose compromises hurt the family of someone I now consider to be my own family. It's easy to subtly shift our convictions to go with the flow. But don't do it. Don't make some future Christian generation have to leave your name out when they tell your stories because of how something you did tarnished the name of Christ.[35]

5. It's a sad but true fact of life that even one act of compromise can tarnish the name of Christ. How do you want the future generations in your world—like your children or grandchildren—to remember you? What decisions are you making in the here and now to ensure that these future generations will remember you in that way?

Redemption-Displaying

Picture a mountain stream carving its way downward. Most of the water follows the pull of gravity and rushes along the easiest path. But every so often, something surprising happens. A trickle seeps upward through cracks, defying gravity, curving around obstacles in unexpected ways. These rare movements stand out because they break the expected pattern.

Displaying grace is just as striking. It flows against the current of the world, disrupting the usual equations of merit and reward. The world operates on straightforward principles—work hard, earn success; make mistakes, face consequences. Certainly, these are not bad principles in and of themselves. But as followers of Christ, we are called to break this rhythm at times. We are to interrupt the natural flow with moments of unexpected grace—choosing generosity over advantage, mercy over retaliation, and service over self-interest.

Again, this doesn't mean we abandon sound business practices or ignore consequences. Just as water still flows downhill, businesses must operate on merit, competition, and fair exchange. But, like water defying gravity, grace disrupts the natural flow of self-interest. It makes people stop and wonder: *What kind of force drives someone to act this way?*

Grace that flows against the current of this world can take many forms. It could mean taking responsibility for a colleague's mistake. It could mean giving a friend a second chance instead of giving them an I-told-you-so speech. It could mean investing in someone who has nothing to offer you in return. These aren't just acts of kindness. They are *tangible reflections* of the grace you have received in Christ. When you extend grace in unexpected ways, you mirror the very pattern of God's love toward you.

Jesus' grace toward you is shocking because it is completely undeserved. In the same way, your grace will be most visible when it disrupts the normal expectations of human behavior. Each time you move against the gravitational pull of self-interest, you create an opportunity to point to the ultimate Source of this countercultural flow.

Grace comes with a cost. Like water moving uphill, it takes effort, sacrifice, and a willingness to defy the world's logic. However, as you consider the cost, you can know that every act of grace—big or small—serves as a signpost that points others to the greatest act of grace the world has ever known. So . . . what kind of grace will flow from you today?

Read | 1 Peter 2:19–23; Colossians 3:13; Matthew 5:38–42

1. How does Peter connect your response to unfair treatment with Jesus' example in 1 Peter 2:19–23? What might this look like in your workplace or in another area of life?

2. Paul instructs us in Colossians 3:13 to "bear with each other and forgive one another if any of you has a grievance." What relationship in your life currently requires you to "bear with" difficult behavior or personality differences? How might practicing the patient love that Paul encourages in this verse help you reflect Jesus to that person?

We serve a King from beyond the world. A King who, unlike Nebuchad-nezzar, leveraged his resources to serve us, not for us to serve him (see Matthew 20:28). The Nebuchadnezzars of the world are usually big on taxation, self-promotion, and double standards. Our King took upon himself the form of a servant so that he could redeem his subjects who had betrayed and deserted him. Few things demonstrate the distinction between the kingdoms of Babylon and the kingdom of Christ quite so poignantly as *grace*. Thus, it shouldn't be surprising that a sovereign God arranges circumstances in which we are wronged and disadvantaged so that we can display his kind of grace.[36]

3. You *always* have the opportunity to display grace. But do you? Check the box next to the answer below that represents how you most typically respond in each situation.

When treated unfairly, I usually . . .
- ☐ Retaliate
- ☐ Ignore the person
- ☐ Respond with grace

When given the opportunity to help, I generally . . .
- ☐ Calculate the cost of helping
- ☐ Sometimes help, if it's convenient
- ☐ Respond generously

When wronged by a friend or coworker, I tend to . . .
- ☐ Seek justice
- ☐ Let it go
- ☐ Seek restoration

4. Jesus' command to "go two miles" in his teaching found in Matthew 5:38–42 references Roman law allowing soldiers to force civilians to carry their equipment one mile. What "forced mile" are you currently walking in your life (like an unwanted obligation or imposition)? How might voluntarily going the "second mile" transform this situation?

Living out the gospel in our lives does *not* mean merely throwing in a few sporadic moments of grace in an otherwise self-interested pursuit of accumulation. A gospel-shaped approach to our lives goes much deeper than that. It means reshaping our whole approach to our lives and careers according to Jesus' example of servanthood—coming not to be served, but to serve. "When you give a dinner or a banquet," Jesus says, "do not invite your friends or your brothers or your relatives or rich neighbors, lest they also invite you in return and you be repaid. But when you give a feast, invite the poor, the crippled, the lame, the blind, and you will be blessed, because they cannot repay you" (Luke 14:12–14 ESV). Jesus is using "banquet" as a metaphor for our lives. "If your life is a party," he's asking, "who are you throwing it for?"[37]

5. There is a big difference between "throwing in a few sporadic moments of grace" and "reshaping our whole approach to our lives and careers" according to Jesus' model of servanthood. How do you define the difference between the two in your life? What would it take for you to move closer to Jesus' model of servanthood?

Mission-Advancing

Championship teams aren't built on talent alone. They thrive because of role players—the ones who push in practice, mentor behind the scenes, and specialize in key moments. Without these role players, even the brightest stars can't win. The player who never sees game time but sharpens the starters in practice, the veteran who steadies the locker room, the specialist who steps in for a single clutch play—each one advances the team's mission. Without their contributions, the team would not reach its full potential.

In the same way, God's mission doesn't advance through superstars alone. It moves forward through everyday faithfulness in unseen places. When we grasp this, it transforms how we view our work. Our role, no matter how small it might seem from our vantage point, is a *vital* part of God's mission. The unseen faithfulness of "ordinary" followers of Christ is just as significant as the visible leadership of pastors or missionaries.

When the Jewish exiles returned to Jerusalem and started rebuilding the temple, they quickly became discouraged. The previous temple, built by Solomon but destroyed by the Babylonians, had been a grand and impressive structure. What they were building paled by comparison. However, God wanted them to know it wasn't the *end result* that mattered but the fact they were *honoring him* by making the temple a priority. He said to them, "The glory of this present house will be greater than the glory of the former house" (Haggai 2:9).

We often picture mission work as crossing oceans or doing something for the Lord that others will deem grand, spectacular, and impressive. But what God is saying is that some of the most important mission fields are the cubicle next door, or the gym where you work out, or the coffee shop where you study. These are places where trust builds over time, where relationships naturally form, and where God can use you in ways you don't recognize.

The question isn't whether you're advancing God's mission but how intentionally you're doing it. Every player shapes a team's culture, for better or worse. Likewise, every Christian either advances or hinders God's mission through their daily choices and interactions. When you embrace this reality, even routine tasks become opportunities for kingdom impact.

This perspective frees you from the false divide between sacred and secular work. Every task and interaction carries kingdom significance when you realize God's mission moves forward through ordinary people walking in faithfulness. Even when no one else sees . . . God does.

Read | Matthew 28:18–20; 9:35–10:1; 1 Corinthians 9:19–23

1. What are some of the instructions Jesus gave in Matthew 28:18–20 when it comes to making disciples? How can focusing on Jesus' promise to be "with you always" (verse 20) affect your willingness to step into the mission that God has given you?

2. In Matthew 9:35–10:1, the Gospel writer describes Jesus looking at the people and seeing them as "sheep without a shepherd" (verse 36). In response, Jesus does three things: (1) feels deep compassion for them, (2) tells his disciples to pray for workers to reach them, and (3) sends his disciples out to them. Take a moment to reflect on these three areas. Use the scale below to rate how you are doing in each, and then write one practical step you could take this week to grow in the area where you sense the most room for growth.

Compassion for the lost:

1	2	3	4	5	6	7	8	9	10
[needs work]									[doing great]

Praying for the lost:

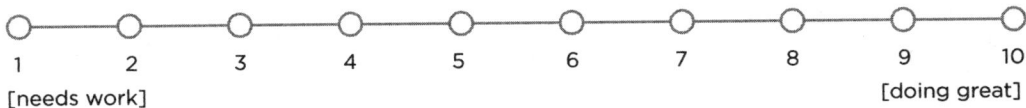

```
O——O——O——O——O——O——O——O——O——O
1    2    3    4    5    6    7    8    9    10
[needs work]                              [doing great]
```

Going to the lost to share Jesus:

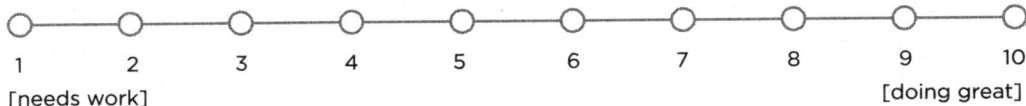

```
O——O——O——O——O——O——O——O——O——O
1    2    3    4    5    6    7    8    9    10
[needs work]                              [doing great]
```

> The Great Commission Jesus gave to the disciples assumes we are already going somewhere. Literally, the original Greek language says "as you are going." It's not just a command for a few of us to *start* going somewhere; it's an acknowledgment that we're *already* headed somewhere. You don't have to hop on a plane to Zambia to engage in the Great Commission. Your work, family, school, neighborhood, and soccer pitch are your mission fields. In fact, you might argue that Christians in the marketplace today have greater access to strategic, unreached places than anyone else! Urbanization, market globalization, and revolutions in technology have given the professional community nearly universal access to people everywhere.[38]

3. *You* have a mission field. It's wherever you live. God may ask you to move to the other side of the world to be a missionary, but your mission field *today* is wherever you do life. Think about how each of the following spheres of your life represents a mission field. Add two more spheres not explicitly mentioned in the text that apply to you specifically.

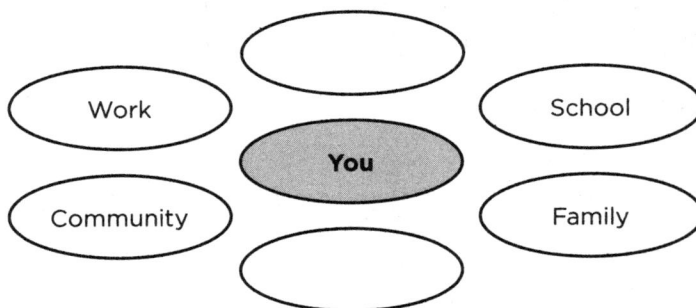

Work   [ ]   School

Community   **You**   Family

[ ]

4. In 1 Corinthians 9:19–23, Paul explains how he became "all things" to all people to reach as many as possible. How could you likewise adapt your communication style or approach to better connect with different groups of people in your life? What personal freedoms or preferences might God be asking you to set aside to better connect with them?

You've got to get a job *somewhere*. So why not get a job in a place where you can be part of something King Jesus is doing? Remember, you're just an exile here. So arrange your life according to what is most advantageous for Jesus' kingdom. If you have freedom to move around in Babylon, you should make those moves based on what is in the best interests of your home country. God wants his people to put down roots in Babylons around the world, to get jobs there, to be spooky good at those jobs and then leverage the opportunities provided by those jobs to point people to Jesus.[39]

5. What "spooky good" talents has God given you that could be strategically used for his kingdom? Are you currently positioning yourself to maximize their kingdom impact? If not, what is one step you could take this week toward using that ability for God?

Connect and Discuss

Take some time today to connect with a fellow group member and discuss some of the key insights from this session. Use any of the following prompts to help guide your discussion.

What did you like best from the content in this session, including both the group study and personal study? Why?

In what ways do you face pressure in your work (or other areas of life) to compromise your integrity? How did what you learned this last week help you to rethink how to handle it?

Where in your life do you sometimes receive unfair treatment? In the past, have you responded with grace? If not, how could you do so in the future?

What would it look like to make your job primarily about advancing Jesus' mission? What is one change you could make to move in that direction?

What do you feel most excited to explore in the session ahead? Why?

Catch Up and Read Ahead

Use this time to go back and complete any of the study and reflection questions from previous days that you weren't able to finish. Make a note below of any revelations you've had and reflect on any growth or personal insights you've gained.

Read chapters 13–17 in *Everyday Revolutionary* before the next group gathering. Use the space below to make note of anything in those chapters that stands out to you or encourages you.

BEFORE GROUP MEETING	Read chapters 13–17 in *Everyday Revolutionary*
	Read the Welcome section (page 114)

GROUP MEETING	Discuss the Connect questions
	Watch the video teaching for session 6
	Discuss the questions that follow as a group
	Do the closing exercise and pray (pages 114–118)

STUDY 1	Complete the personal study (pages 120–123)
STUDY 2	Complete the personal study (pages 124–127)
STUDY 3	Complete the personal study (pages 128–131)

CONNECT AND DISCUSS	Connect with one or two group members
	Discuss the follow-up questions (page 132)

WRAP IT UP	Complete any unfinished personal studies (page 133)
	Connect with your group about the next study that you want to go through together

Testify Loudly

*Come and hear, all you who fear God; let
me tell you what he has done for me.*

PSALM 66:16

WELCOME [READ ON YOUR OWN]

Picture a lighthouse during a fierce storm. Though it gets battered by wind and waves, it stands firm, rooted in bedrock. What really sets a lighthouse apart isn't just its strength. It's the bright beam it sends across dark waters that guides ships to safety. This lighthouse image gives us a picture of our testimony in today's world. The unyielding structure represents courage—the willingness to stand firm when powerful cultural currents push against us. Not because we're stubborn, but because we're anchored to something solid—or Some*one*.

Meanwhile, the inviting light represents joy. It's that unexplainable delight that radiates from believers even in the toughest of times. This is not fake happiness that ignores problems. Rather, it a deep confidence and conviction we hold that there's more to the story than what's visible in the storm. It's the kind of joy that makes sailors look twice and wonder, "How can that light shine so steadily when everything around it is chaos?"

When these two elements work together—courage and joy—something remarkable occurs. A lighthouse without light doesn't help anyone navigate. A bright light that moves with every wind just creates confusion. But unwavering courage combined with genuine joy? That stops people in their tracks and makes them wonder what's going on. It creates questions that open doors to conversations about the foundation of our hope.

In our increasingly skeptical society, what truly captures people's attention isn't clever arguments for faith but lives that demonstrate both firm conviction and unexpected joy. When we hold to biblical truths that may be unpopular while radiating genuine joy that hardship can't extinguish, people inevitably get curious about the source.

This final session explores how to "testify loudly" through courage that won't bend and joy that won't dim—even when it costs us. These bold expressions point people directly to Jesus, the ultimate Source of both our stability and our light.

CONNECT [10 MINUTES]

Get the session started by choosing one or both of the following questions to discuss together as a group.

- What is something that spoke to you in last week's personal study that you would like to share with the group?

— *or* —

- What brings you the deepest joy in your life? How do people around you respond when they see this joy in you?

WATCH [25 MINUTES]

Now watch the video for this session. Below is an outline of the main points covered during the teaching. Record any key concepts that stand out to you.

OUTLINE

I. "Living quietly" and "testifying loudly" work together in our Christian witness.
   A. Living quietly sets the stage for testifying loudly.
   B. Peter says our lives should compel others to ask about our hope.
   C. When we testify loudly, God often amplifies our witness with his power.

II. Loud courage demonstrates our ultimate allegiance to Christ.
   A. Daniel's three friends (Shadrach, Meshach, and Abednego) became famous for refusing to bow down to Nebuchadnezzar's statue.
   B. Christians under Diocletian's persecution refused to say, "Caesar is Lord."
   C. Persecution rarely comes because of private religious practices.
   D. Compromise, not persecution, poses the greatest threat to the church.

III. Loud joy testifies to our hope even in difficult circumstances.
   A. Paul and Silas sang hymns with joy in spite of being imprisoned.
   B. Their unexplainable joy got the attention of the Philippian jailer.
   C. Joy during suffering points to a hope that others want to understand.
   D. Our joy in hardship creates opportunities to point to Christ as our treasure.

IV. When heaven gets loud, God validates our testimony.
   A. Throughout Daniel's time in Babylon, God showed up in supernatural ways.
   B. Daniel's ability to interpret Nebuchadnezzar's dream demonstrated God's power.
   C. James teaches that Elijah's experience with answered prayer is available to all believers in Christ.
   D. We can expect God to occasionally break in as our culture becomes more post-Christian.

NOTES

DISCUSS [35 MINUTES]

Discuss what you just watched by answering the following questions.

1. There are four ways that Christians can testify loudly: (1) through courage, (2) through joy, (3) through generosity, and (4) through hospitality. Which of these do you find most natural to express? Which requires the most effort? Explain your response.

2. Invite someone to read Daniel 3:16–18. What strikes you about the response of Shadrach, Meshach, and Abednego to Nebuchadnezzar's threat? What do you learn from their example about how to stand strong when facing pressure to compromise?

3. Paul and Silas's joy in prison, as recorded in Acts 16:16–34, caught the attention of the Philippian jailer and resulted in him coming to salvation in Christ. Have you ever witnessed someone who, like Paul and Silas, maintained their joy even in the face of suffering? If so, what impact did that have on you or others who observed it?

4. Ask someone to read aloud 1 Peter 3:15–16. What does Peter say you should be prepared to do when people ask why you have chosen to follow Christ? What does it mean to do this—to give your testimony—"with gentleness and respect"?

5. As our culture becomes more post-Christian, we shouldn't be surprised to see God "get loud" through supernatural interventions. What is your reaction to this idea? Have you ever witnessed or experienced God validating someone's testimony in a supernatural way? If so, what was that experience like for you?

RESPOND [10 MINUTES]

As a follower of Jesus, you are called to "testify loudly." You do this not only through the words you speak but also the actions you take—and always with gentleness and respect. Take a few minutes to reflect on this idea as you read the following passage and answer the questions.

> [The Jewish elders and teachers of the law] called them in again and commanded them not to speak or teach at all in the name of Jesus. But Peter and John replied, "Which is right in God's eyes: to listen to you, or to him? You be the judges! As for us, we cannot help speaking about what we have seen and heard." After further threats they let them go. They could not decide how to punish them, because all the people were praising God for what had happened.
>
> ACTS 4:18-21

How did Peter and John demonstrate the practice of testifying loudly in this passage? How did they demonstrate courage in their profession of Christ?

What was the end result of Peter and John's act of "loud courage"? What does this say about the way in which God honors our obedience in telling others about Jesus?

PRAY [10 MINUTES]

As you close, pray for wisdom and courage to live as an everyday revolutionary. Ask God to help you transcend the culture war mentality while representing his kingdom. Pray for opportunities to demonstrate loud courage, joy, generosity, and hospitality in ways that prompt others to ask about your hope. Ask for the Holy Spirit's power to strengthen you when you face pressure to compromise and for discernment to recognize when God is validating your testimony in supernatural ways. Finally, pray that your quiet lives and loud testimony will represent Jesus to your Babylon and point others to his lordship and coming kingdom.

Personal Study

The last two weeks have focused on living quietly, but sometimes you need to speak up and vocally tell others about God and about Jesus. When you were little, maybe you can remember your mom saying, "Use your words." There are certainly times when you need to use your words to point people to God's truth and love—and to the gospel. So, in this personal study, you will explore five ways to testify loudly. As you work through each of these exercises, continue to record your responses, insights, and key takeaways. If you are reading *Everyday Revolutionary* alongside this study, first review chapters 13–17 of the book.

Loud Courage and Loud Joy

In 2010, Joni Eareckson Tada, a well-known Christian author and speaker, faced a new battle that tested her faith in a profound way. Joni, who had already endured the challenges of being a quadriplegic for more than fifty years following a diving accident, was now confronted with a fresh storm: *cancer*. For most, this would be a crushing blow. Yet in the face of this new diagnosis, Joni's response was not one of despair but of remarkable courage and joy.

Despite the grueling treatments, uncertainty, and weight of her diagnosis, Joni didn't retreat from her faith. Instead, she shared her journey openly, posting on social media, "I don't think I'll ever get over the fact that I'm in the hands of the One who made me, and He will carry me all the way through. This is my joy, and it's my strength."

Joni exemplified the kind of joy that doesn't depend on circumstances but is rooted in trust and hope in God. Her joy wasn't for her alone. It became a living, breathing testimony to the power of God's presence. People from all over the world reached out to Joni, amazed by the strength and peace she radiated in the face of such overwhelming trials. Many who didn't know Christ saw her unwavering hope and were drawn to the Savior who gave her that peace. Her joy in suffering was a beacon of the love and power of Jesus.[40]

As followers of Christ, we aren't called to wait for easy circumstances before we express joy. In fact, it's often in the hardest moments that the joy of the Lord shines the brightest. The Bible tells us, "Consider it pure joy, my brothers and sisters, whenever you face trials of many kinds" (James 1:2). True joy doesn't mean the absence of pain. It means choosing to trust in God's goodness, even when everything around us is uncertain.

Joni's story is a powerful example of this kind of joy—a joy that comes not from our circumstances but from the confidence that God is with us in the midst of them. When we choose to live out this kind of joy, it doesn't just change us; it becomes a testimony to others. As we endure trials with joy, we become living proof of the hope found in Jesus, showing the world a peace that surpasses understanding.

Read | Acts 16:16–21, 22–34; Philippians 1:12–14

1. In Acts 16:16–21, the slave owners were earning a great deal of money from the girl in their possession. Paul would have understood these owners wanted to protect their profits. Given this, how does what he did represent an act of loud courage?

2. After Paul and Silas were imprisoned, they prayed and sang hymns (see Acts 16:22–34). What impact did their courageous joy in suffering have on the other prisoners? What does this say about the impact your courageous joy in suffering can have on others?

I've often wondered: Why didn't Paul see the earthquake as God's miraculous provision in setting him free? Paul perceived that God was doing something bigger and better in his situation. God hadn't sent Paul to Philippi just to set him free but to testify loudly to a city full of captives that God could set them free too. The best way Paul could testify to that was by refusing to take advantage of his "miracle" and focus instead on the soul of the Philippian jailor. Paul won him not through philosophical argumentation but through joy and generosity in the midst of persecution.[41]

3. Is there a situation in your life right now where you need to choose courageous joy? If so, what are three practical steps you could take to face that fear with both courage and joy?

Step #1:

Step #2:

Step #3:

4. In Philippians 1:12–14, the apostle Paul writes how he discovered purpose in his struggles by seeing how they advanced God's mission. How might that same perspective shift the way that you view your challenges? How could your difficulties become a platform for sharing your faith?

It's awesome when God shows off his miraculous power by answering a prayer in a miraculous way. But it's sometimes even more attention-grabbing when we show off his inestimable worth by remaining joyful in him even when he doesn't answer prayer in that way. It's when everything in your life goes wrong and that smile stays on your face that the world pays attention. I'm not trying to say God never brings glory to himself through miraculous provision. I'm saying that what gets a cynical world's attention the most quickly is when a Christian possesses unshakable joy even when everything goes wrong. That alerts them to the reality of another even more real and even more important world than the Babylon they see in front of them.[42]

5. How do you respond to the statement, "It's when everything in your life goes wrong and that smile stays on your face that the world pays attention"? Does that kind of joy feel possible to you? Have you seen it in others? If so, what did their example teach you?

Loud Generosity and Loud Hospitality

The city of Carthage was in chaos. The year was AD 251, and a devastating plague was sweeping through the streets. Bodies piled up as fear-stricken citizens fled, abandoning even their own family members to die. Yet while most ran for safety, one group stayed behind: the Christians.

Though mocked by critics such as Celsus, a philosopher, for being weak and insignificant, these believers risked their lives to care for the sick, bury the dead, and offer comfort to the dying. In their supposed weakness, they displayed a strength the world couldn't ignore.

This moment in history reveals a powerful truth: Generosity and hospitality together create something greater than either can alone. Generosity without hospitality can feel impersonal—like dropping off supplies but keeping a safe distance. Hospitality without generosity can feel superficial—like welcoming someone in but holding back real sacrifice. But when combined, they form a testimony that is impossible to explain away.

Consider how this plays out today. A family doesn't just deliver groceries to elderly neighbors (generosity) but also invites them to dinner (hospitality). A professional offers free career mentoring (generosity), but instead of just emailing advice, he or she shares meals and real-life wisdom (hospitality). A church assists refugee families (generosity), but the members also open their homes to build lasting friendships (hospitality).

These combinations create what sociologists call "thick relationships"—meaningful bonds that go beyond polite exchanges. In an isolated world where neighbors often remain strangers, these relationships shine all the brighter. They whisper of a kingdom where love isn't transactional and where people matter beyond what they can offer in return.

Generosity opens doors. Hospitality walks through them. Together, they stir questions our culture struggles to answer: *Why would someone give with no expectation of return? Why would they open up their private spaces to strangers?* This is where our witness speaks loudest—not through polished arguments but through lives that echo God's heart. He is not generous from a distance. He draws near. He doesn't just give good gifts. He invites us into relationship.

So, how might you embody loud generosity and loud hospitality this week? Who in your life needs both your giving and your presence? The beauty of this calling is that it doesn't require wealth, status, or power— just a heart willing to open both hands and doors.

Read | Luke 10:30–37; Acts 2:44–47; 1 Peter 4:8–10

1. The Samaritan in Jesus' parable provided immediate help but also made long-term arrangements for the man's care (see Luke 10:30–37). What does this demonstrate about Jesus' call for his disciples to extend both generosity and hospitality?

2. In Acts 2:44–47, we read how the early believers held all things in common and shared their possessions. What specific resources (time, skills, home, finances) might God be calling you to share more generously with others in your faith community? Is there a way you can be more generous with one of your resources this week?

> Uniquely Christian generosity mimics the sacrifice Jesus made for us. Others perceive in our actions the beauty of some scene precious to us that we long to recreate—the echo of a tune we want to hear played again. It's been said that those who believe the gospel inevitably become like the gospel. They can't help it! There is simply no way to experience the extraordinary generosity of the gospel and not become extraordinarily generous yourself. It becomes a tune you have to play, an instinct you can't ignore. It's more than just a general disposition to "niceness"—it's a taste for radical generosity that breaks through every once in a while in your own behavior.[43]

3. As a Christian, you have experienced God's extraordinary generosity, and thus he asks you to likewise become extraordinarily generous. God is calling you to "loud hospitality." How are you doing with that calling? Conduct a brief hospitality audit.

Current practices: What am I already doing? Who do I regularly welcome?

Available resources: What could I share? What spaces could I open?

Barriers: What holds me back? What fears do I have?

> **Next steps:** What next step could I take? What relationship could I build?

4. What would it look like for your church community to be marked by earnest love, open hospitality, and joyful service (see 1 Peter 4:8–10)? How might you lead the way and help to make that vision a reality?

In a sometimes-hostile culture, our homes are often the most valuable tools we have for engaging others with the gospel. Author Rosaria Butterfield says, "Stop thinking of witnessing to your neighbors as sneaky evangelistic raids into their sinful lives. . . . For words to be persuasive, they can't be stronger than relationships."[44] Many people have no interest in hearing an evangelistic presentation, no matter how compellingly it's presented. The truth is, they see our eloquent confidence as part of the problem! So, how do we make space for God-talk in such an emotionally charged atmosphere? The same way Jesus did: by sitting around tables, eating and drinking together.[45]

5. Our homes are often "the most valuable tools we have for engaging others with the gospel." How might viewing your home as a mission tool change how you use your living space? What is one step you could take this week to move in that direction?

Heaven Gets Loud

Under the cover of night in Iran, where converting to Christianity can mean prison—or worse—a man sleeps restlessly. Suddenly, a vision breaks through the darkness. A radiant figure appears, his presence unmistakably powerful. "I am the way, the truth, and the life," he says, handing the man a Bible. The dream leaves him shaken, yet undeniably drawn to Christ. Against all logic, he begins secretly seeking the God he once opposed.

This story is not unique. All across nations hostile to the gospel, similar encounters are reported—visions of Jesus, dreams that awaken faith, supernatural moments that defy human understanding.[46] In places where following Christ carries the highest cost, heaven often gets loud. When human voices must whisper their faith, divine voices frequently thunder.

History tells us the same story. In Babylon, Daniel stood before a hostile king, interpreting dreams that pointed to God's dominion. In the Roman Empire, Paul received divine visions that led him to new mission fields despite fierce resistance. Again and again, when the gospel met opposition, God validated the testimony of his people in remarkable ways.

This doesn't mean we should expect or demand supernatural signs. But it does mean we shouldn't be surprised when God chooses to work in this way—especially where the gospel is least known or most opposed. These divine affirmations often come not through spectacular public displays but through personal encounters: a dream that reveals hidden truth, a prayer that receives an unexpected answer, a word of knowledge that pierces the heart.

At first glance, our secular workplaces or campuses might seem far removed from ancient Babylon or modern-day Iran. But we *will* find ourselves in situations where, like Daniel, we need heaven's validation of our witness. This isn't about seeking signs to bolster our own faith. It's about being open to how God might confirm his reality to those around us.

Such openness requires both boldness and humility—boldness to ask God to work powerfully through us and humility to recognize that any supernatural confirmation comes from him, not us. It means praying for the sick colleague, speaking truth to the troubled friend, sharing an insight God places on our hearts—always pointing to Jesus as the source.

So dare to live out your faith audaciously. Extend radical generosity and heartfelt hospitality wherever you see a need. For through your actions, the quiet whispers of heaven may become a resounding chorus in your world.

Read | Daniel 2:27–30; Acts 2:1–9; 16:6–10

1. When Daniel stood before Nebuchadnezzar to interpret his dream, he knew that lives—including his own—were at stake (see Daniel 2:27–30). Yet he responded with both humility and bold confidence in God's revelation. How did Daniel strike that balance? What do you learn from his example about speaking truth with humility and courage?

2. In Acts 2:1–9, God empowered the believers to speak in a way that left the crowd bewildered and amazed. When was the last time someone was genuinely curious or surprised because of your faith? What could you do to open yourself to God's transforming work so that your life stirs up that same kind of holy curiosity in others?

I love the phrase, "But there is a God in heaven who reveals mysteries" (Daniel 2:28). Daniel was explaining to Nebuchadnezzar that God was showing him who he was by doing things that only he could do. It was a divine affirmation of Daniel's testimony. God puts his people into impossible situations *to show there is a God in heaven*. Sometimes he does that by giving us codes to live by that set us apart. Sometimes he does that by making us prosper as we abide by that code. Sometimes he does so through our indomitable joy in suffering or our refusal to compromise our convictions because of our certainty of a greater and more permanent treasure in him. Sometimes he does it through our radical generosity on display. And sometimes he does it by breaking into an impossible situation with something only he can do.[47]

3. The Lord sometimes puts his people into impossible situations to show "there is a God in heaven." Share an example of how you have seen God work in the following ways:

Through prayer:	
Through provision:	
Through protection:	

4. In Acts 16:6–10, Paul received a vision of a man from Macedonia who cried out for the missionaries to come and help him. If God gave you such a "Macedonian vision" today:

> Do you think you would recognize it? Why or why not?

> Would you be ready to respond immediately? Why or why not?

> In light of this, what might help you stay spiritually tuned in to hear God's call?

Don't write off God's heavenly affirmations as a thing of the past. Yearn for them. Ask for them. Receiving heavenly affirmation is part of what it means to shine like the stars in the sky. Supernatural "signatures" testify that there actually is a God in heaven—a God who is real, a God who loves and who listens, a God who is returning again for his people. So step out there and give God a chance to shine through you.[48]

5. Consider this idea of asking for and yearning for heavenly affirmations. What types of heavenly affirmations would you like to receive? How will you ask for those today?

Connect and Discuss

Take some time today to connect with a fellow group member and discuss some of the key insights from this session. Use any of the following prompts to help guide your discussion.

What did you like best from the overall content from this course—including both the group study and personal study? Why?

Do you have any opportunities coming up to display courageous joy in difficult circumstances? If so, how can you pray together for that?

Do you find it more difficult to practice generosity or hospitality? What makes it difficult for you? What would help the most in this?

Have you ever experienced God "speaking loudly" to affirm who he is or what he has said? If so, what was that experience like?

What is one thing from this study that you will actively apply to your life?

Wrap It Up

Use this time to go back and complete any of the study and reflection questions from previous days that you weren't able to finish. Make a note below of any questions you've had and reflect on any growth or personal insights you've gained.

Finally, discuss with your group what studies you might want to go through next and when you will plan on meeting together again to study God's Word.

Leader's Guide

Thank you for your willingness to lead your group through this study! What you have chosen to do is valuable and will make a difference in the lives of others. *Everyday Revolutionary* is a six-session Bible study built around video content and small-group interaction. As the group leader, imagine yourself as the host of a party. Your job is to take care of your guests by managing the details so that when your guests arrive, they can focus on one another and on the interaction around the topic for that session.

Your role as the group leader is not to answer all the questions or reteach the content—the video, book, and study guide will do most of that work. Your job is to guide the experience and cultivate your small group into a connected and engaged community. This will make it a place for members to process, question, and reflect—not necessarily to receive more instruction. There are several elements in this leader's guide that will help you as you structure your study and reflection time, so be sure to follow along and take advantage of each one.

BEFORE YOU BEGIN

Before your first meeting, make sure the group members have a copy of this study guide. Alternately, you can hand out the study guides at your first meeting and give the members some time to look over the material and ask any preliminary questions. Also, make sure that the group members are aware they have access to the streaming videos at any time by following the instructions provided with this guide. During your first meeting, ask the members to provide their names, phone numbers, and email addresses so that you can keep in touch.

Generally, the ideal size for a group is eight to ten people, which will ensure that everyone has enough time to participate in discussions. If you have more people, break up the main group into smaller subgroups. Encourage those who show up at the first meeting to commit to attending the duration of the study, as this will help the group members get to know one another, create stability for the group, and help you know how best to prepare to lead the participants through the material.

Each session begins with an opening reflection in the Welcome section. The questions that follow in the Connect section serve as icebreakers to get the group members thinking about the topic. In the rest of the study, it's generally not a good idea to have everyone answer every question—a free-flowing discussion is more desirable. But with the icebreaker question, you can go around the circle and ask each person to respond. Encourage shy people to share, but don't force them.

At your first meeting, let the group members know that each session also contains a personal study section they can use to continue to engage with the content until the next meeting. While doing this section is optional, it will help them cement the concepts presented during the group study time.

Let them know that if they choose to do so, they can watch the video for the next session by accessing the streaming code provided with this study guide. Invite them to bring any questions and insights to your next meeting, especially if they had a breakthrough moment or didn't understand something.

PREPARATION FOR EACH SESSION

As the leader, there are a few things you should do to best prepare for each meeting:

- **Read through the session.** This will help you become more familiar with the content and know how to structure the discussion times.

- **Decide how the videos will be used.** Determine whether you want the members to watch the videos ahead of time (again, via the streaming access code provided with this study guide) or together as a group.

- **Decide which questions you want to discuss.** Based on the length of your group discussions, you may not be able to get through all the questions. So look over the discussion questions provided in each session and mark which ones you definitely want to cover.

- **Be familiar with the questions you want to discuss.** When the group meets, you'll be watching the clock, so make sure you are familiar with the questions you have selected.

- **Pray for your group.** Pray for your group members and ask God to lead them as they study his Word and listen to his Spirit.

In many cases, there will be no one "right" answer to the questions. Answers will vary, especially when the group members are sharing their personal experiences.

STRUCTURING THE DISCUSSION TIME

You will need to determine with your group how long you want your meetings to last so that you can plan your time accordingly. Suggested times for each section have been provided in this study guide, and if you adhere to these times, your group will meet for ninety minutes. However, many groups like to meet for two hours. If this describes your particular group, follow the times listed in the right-hand column of the chart given below.

SECTION	90 Minutes	120 Minutes
CONNECT (discuss one or more of the opening questions for the session)	15 minutes	20 minutes
WATCH (watch the teaching material together and take notes)	20 minutes	20 minutes
DISCUSS (discuss the study questions you selected ahead of time)	35 minutes	50 minutes
RESPOND (write down key takeaways)	10 minutes	15 minutes
PRAY (pray together and dismiss)	10 minutes	15 minutes

As the group leader, it is up to you to keep track of the time and to keep things on schedule. You might want to set a timer for each segment so that both you and the group members know when the time is up. (There are some good phone apps for timers that play a gentle chime or other pleasant sound instead of a disruptive noise.)

Don't be concerned if group members are quiet or slow to share. People are often quiet when they are pulling together their ideas, and this might be a new experience for some of them. Just ask a question and let it hang in the air until someone shares. You can then say, "Thank you. What about others? What came to you when you watched that portion of the teaching?"

GROUP DYNAMICS

Leading a group through *Everyday Revolutionary* will prove to be highly rewarding both to you and your group members. But you still may encounter challenges along the way! Discussions can get off track. Group members may not be sensitive to the needs and ideas of others.

Some might worry that they will be expected to talk about matters that make them feel awkward. Others may express comments that result in disagreements.

To help ease this strain on you and the group, consider the following ground rules:

- When someone raises a question or comment that is off the main topic, suggest you deal with it another time, or, if you feel led to go in that direction, let the group know that you will be spending some time discussing it.

- If someone asks a question that you don't know how to answer, admit it and move on. At your discretion, feel free to invite group members to comment on questions that call for personal experience.

- If you find that one or two people are dominating the discussion time, direct a few questions to others in the group. Outside the main group time, ask the more dominating members to help you draw out the quieter ones. Work to make them part of the solution instead of part of the problem.

- When a disagreement occurs, encourage the group members to process the matter in love. Encourage those on opposite sides to restate what they heard the other side say about the matter, and then invite each side to evaluate if that perception is accurate. Lead the group in examining other passages related to the topic and look for common ground.

When any of these issues arise, encourage the members of your group to follow these words from Scripture: "Love one another" (John 13:34); "If it is possible, as far as it depends on you, live at peace with everyone" (Romans 12:18); "Whatever is true . . . noble . . . right . . . pure . . . lovely . . . if anything is excellent or praiseworthy—think about such things" (Philippians 4:8); and, "Everyone should be quick to listen, slow to speak and slow to become angry" (James 1:19). This will make your group time more rewarding and beneficial for everyone who attends.

Thank you for taking the time to lead your group. You are making a difference in your members' lives and having an impact on their journey toward a better understanding of what it means to transcend the culture war and transform the world for Christ.

Notes

1. Makoto Fujimura, *Culture Care: Reconnecting with Beauty for Our Common Life* (IVP Books, 2017).
2. J. D. Greear, *Everyday Revolutionary: How to Transcend the Culture War and Transform the World* (Zondervan, 2025), chapter 1.
3. Greear, *Everyday Revolutionary,* chapter 1.
4. Greear, *Everyday Revolutionary,* chapter 2.
5. Greear, *Everyday Revolutionary,* chapter 2.
6. Greear, *Everyday Revolutionary,* chapter 3.
7. Greear, *Everyday Revolutionary,* chapter 3.
8. Wangari Maathai, "I Will Be a Hummingbird," https://thekidshouldseethis.com/post/wangari-maathai-i-will-be-a-hummingbird.
9. Greear, *Everyday Revolutionary,* chapter 4.
10. Greear, *Everyday Revolutionary,* chapter 4.
11. Greear, *Everyday Revolutionary,* chapter 5.
12. Greear, *Everyday Revolutionary,* chapter 5.
13. Dawson Trotman, *Born to Reproduce* (The Navigators, 1955).
14. Greear, *Everyday Revolutionary,* chapter 6.
15. Greear, *Everyday Revolutionary,* chapter 6.
16. Nathan A. Finn, "Missionaries You Should Know: William Carey," International Mission Board, July 31, 2018, https://www.imb.org/2018/07/31/missionaries-you-should-know-william-carey/.
17. J. D. Greear, from a message titled "An Alternative Political Gospel," 2025.
18. Greear, "An Alternative Political Gospel."
19. Greear, "An Alternative Political Gospel."
20. Greear, "An Alternative Political Gospel."
21. Greear, "An Alternative Political Gospel."
22. Greear, "An Alternative Political Gospel."
23. Dorothy Sayers, "Why Work?", from *Letters to the Diminished Church* (W Publishing, 2007).
24. Sayers, "Why Work?"
25. Sayers, "Why Work?"

26. Greear, *Everyday Revolutionary,* part 2.
27. Greear, *Everyday Revolutionary,* chapter 8.
28. Greear, *Everyday Revolutionary,* chapter 8.
29. Greear, *Everyday Revolutionary,* chapter 8.
30. Greear, *Everyday Revolutionary,* chapter 9.
31. Greear, *Everyday Revolutionary,* chapter 9.
32. Philip Yancey and Paul Brand, "Members of the Body: Reflections of Dr. Paul Brand," BioLogos, February 12, 2020, https://biologos.org/articles/members-of-the-body-reflections-of-dr-paul-brand.
33. Paul Brand, *Pain: The Gift Nobody Wants: A Surgeon's Journey of Discovery* (HarperCollins, 1994).
34. Greear, *Everyday Revolutionary,* chapter 10.
35. Greear, *Everyday Revolutionary,* chapter 10.
36. Greear, *Everyday Revolutionary,* chapter 11.
37. Greear, *Everyday Revolutionary,* chapter 11.
38. Greear, *Everyday Revolutionary,* chapter 12.
39. Greear, *Everyday Revolutionary,* chapter 12.
40. Joni and Friends, "Joni Eareckson Tada Receives New Cancer Diagnosis," Joni & Friends, November 19, 2018, https://joniandfriends.org/press-releases/new-cancer-diagnosis/.
41. Greear, *Everyday Revolutionary,* chapter 14.
42. Greear, *Everyday Revolutionary,* chapter 14.
43. Greear, *Everyday Revolutionary,* chapter 15.
44. Rosaria Butterfield, *The Gospel Comes with a House Key: Practicing Radically Ordinary Hospitality in Our Post-Christian World* (Wheaton: Crossway, 2018), 95.
45. Greear, *Everyday Revolutionary,* chapter 16.
46. Tre Goins-Phillips, "Iranians Meet Jesus in Dreams, Experience Radical Transformation: 'I Saw a Vision of a Man with a White Robe,'" CBN, January 19, 2023, https://cbn.com/news/cwn/iranians-meet-jesus-dreams-experience-radical-transformation-i-saw-vision-man-white-robe.
47. Greear, *Everyday Revolutionary,* chapter 17.
48. Greear, *Everyday Revolutionary,* chapter 17.

ABOUT J. D. GREEAR

J. D. Greear is the pastor of The Summit Church in Raleigh-Durham, North Carolina, which has grown from 300 to more than 14,000 under his leadership. He has a bold vision to plant 1,000 new churches by the year 2050. He has authored several books, including *Twelve Truths and a Lie* (2023), *What Are You Going to Do with Your Life?* (2020), *Not God Enough* (2018), *Stop Asking Jesus into Your Heart* (2013), and *Gospel* (2011). He hosts *Summit Life*, a daily thirty-minute radio broadcast and weekly TV program on 200+ stations nationwide, as well as the impactful *Ask the Pastor* podcast. J. D. completed his PhD in theology at Southeastern Baptist Theological Seminary. He is on the board of directors for Chick-fil-A and recently served as the sixty-third president of the Southern Baptist Convention. He and his wife, Veronica, live in the Research Triangle of Raleigh, North Carolina, with their kids: Kharis, Alethia, Ryah, and Adon.

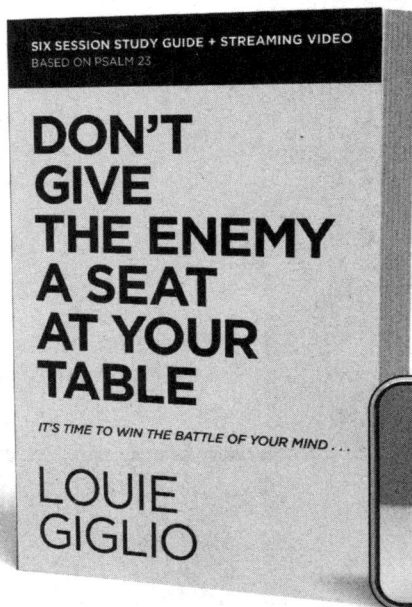